rules

of the game

In an increasingly competitive world, it is quality
of thinking that gives an edge – an idea that opens new
doors, a technique that solves a problem, or an insight
that simply helps make sense of it all.

We work with leading authors in the fields of
management and finance to bring cutting-edge thinking
and best learning practice to a global market.

Under a range of leading imprints, including
Financial Times Prentice Hall, we create world-class
print publications and electronic products giving readers
knowledge and understanding which can then be
applied, whether studying or at work.

To find out more about our business and professional
products, you can visit us at www.business-minds.com

For other Pearson Education publications, visit
www.pearsoned-ema.com

rules
of the game

game

business: a player's guide

Chris Brady and Tara Brady

FINANCIAL TIMES

Prentice Hall

an imprint of Pearson Education

London • New York • San Francisco • Toronto • Sydney • Tokyo • Singapore • Hong Kong

Cape Town • Madrid • Paris • Milan • Munich • Amsterdam

PEARSON EDUCATION LIMITED

Head Office:
Edinburgh Gate
Harlow CM20 2JE
Tel: +44 (0)1279 623623
Fax: +44 (0)1279 431059

London Office:
128 Long Acre
London WC2E 9AN
Tel: +44 (0)20 7447 2000
Fax: +44 (0)20 7240 5771
Website: www.business-minds.com

First published in Great Britain in 2000

© Pearson Education 2000

The right of Chris Brady and Tara Brady to be identified as Author(s)
of this Work has been asserted by them in accordance
with the Copyright, Designs and Patents Act 1988.

ISBN 0 273 64464 5

British Library Cataloguing in Publication Data
A CIP catalogue record for this book can be obtained from the British Library.

10 9 8 7 6 5 4 3 2 1

Designed by Claire Brodmann, Book Designs, Burton-on-Trent
Typeset by Northern Phototypesetting Co. Ltd, Bolton
Printed and bound in Great Britain by Biddles Ltd, Guildford & King's Lynn

The Publishers' policy is to use paper manufactured from sustainable forests.

to Anita

the authors

Chris Brady is currently the Director of Studies for the General Strategic Management MBA at the City University Business School and Head Business Coach at Cape Consulting. He is also a visiting lecturer and adviser on decision-making issues at the Joint Services Command and Staff College, the military's senior staff college. He lectures to the senior staff course of the Kuwaiti Staff College and is a Research Fellow of the Institute of Contemporary British History. He previously served in an intelligence capacity as a Royal Navy officer during the Falklands and Gulf Wars, as well as during the more recent Balkans conflict. He has worked in the gambling and construction industries and also worked for Chryslers in Detroit during his teens. Chris Brady is a qualified UEFA 'A' licence football coach and played and coached football to semi-professional level, which he considers to have been his greatest managerial challenge. He has published on topics as varied as US foreign policy, cabinet government, teamwork, education, the environment, intelligence failures and the United Nations.

Tara C. Brady operates in a business development capacity for Business Process Outsourcing with PricewaterhouseCoopers. He joined the Royal Navy as a junior at 16 and completed a five-year engagement, three of which were aboard HMS *Illustrious*. He spent much of his time there studying. After leaving the Navy he graduated in Business Studies at University of North London before moving to the City with Lloyds of London. Tara Brady has subsequently performed a variety of commercial roles at Sears, NatWest Bank and Guinness before joining his current employers. Extensive experience of studying elite teams (the board) and individuals (functional heads/directors) at close quarters prompted him to create this book on business gaming – what works and does not work. He is a speaker at many commercial conferences and writes for a variety of professional journals. One of his more controversial theories, 'Winning the Battle of Balance', provided a tactical corporate solution to meeting internal clients' requirements whilst maximizing the organizations' needs, an arena in which conflict and game playing is commonplace.

contents

acknowledgments

We apologize for any similarity between our acknowledgements and an Oscar acceptance speech. However, the truth is that many people have contributed to this book, either directly or indirectly, by helping to shape the authors' thinking. The names below, and too many others to mention personally, must be acknowledged. In alphabetical order they are: Stuart Fletcher (Guinness), Nick Ford (PwC), David Gardner (Webperform), Claude Hartridge (PwC), Demis Hassabis (Elixir Studios), Peter Higgins (sportingbet.com), Clive Holtham (City University Business School), Brendan O'Neill (ICI), Michelle Potter (Robinscroft), Ron Noades (Brentford FC), Sionade Robinson (Cape Consulting), General Sir Michael Rose, 'Wild Bill' Stealey (Interactive Magic), Mark Thornton (Pied à Terre), and last, but by no means least, Laura Baldwin, without whom there would be no book.

the state of play

When Sharon Stone famously crossed her legs in *Basic Instinct* she was engaging an even more fundamental instinct – the 'gaming instinct'. She was playing a game into which she had drawn Michael Douglas, whether he knew it or not. She was a game player *par excellence*. Phrases like 'the game's up', 'it's the only game in town', 'play the game', 'don't play games with me', 'the fight game', 'game plan', 'the crying game' are commonplace – games are everywhere. The computer gaming software industry now out-grosses both the film and the music industries. The language of games is so deeply embedded in everyday conversation because it is how we do things. Human beings are innately predisposed to ordering reality using game-like structures – we have a gaming instinct. From trying to arrange your first date to fighting a war there is a generic set of elements to the game that must be understood. In ancient Indian culture the game we now know as snakes and ladders was ritually played as *gyanbaji*, the 'game of knowledge'. It was training for the vagaries of life and a meditation on fatalism. The Indians also designed chess to teach the strategies of war. The game structure describes *any* human interaction, not only the competitive. It includes the collaborative, such as orchestras or plays, and complementary, such as country walking. Winning is viewed as successfully achieving individual potential, as defined by the individual.

We argue in this book that a knowledge of the generic structure of games will, of itself, provide a competitive edge for corporate players. We also believe that a systematic application of that knowledge to any situation can provide a significant competitive advantage. The elements of the game were deduced from a series of interviews with senior management and CEOs in the top 500 companies, and from senior military personnel and top sports people. We asked a simple question: 'If you had to play a game next week, about which you had no foreknowledge, what factors would you consider necessary in order to be successful?' Across the domains the answers converged around five factors. The factors were what we have termed the MORES, which is a mnemonic for **m**otivation – why am I playing; **o**thers – who else is playing; **r**ules – how is the play regulated; **e**nvironment – where am I playing; **s**kills – what skill sets do I need. Analyzing these factors provides basic knowledge of the gaming structure.

Applying knowledge of the MORES to the business game in order to guarantee success requires the player to be competent in three areas – *knowing*, *coaching* and *exploiting*. How much can you know about the MORES; how do you coach yourself and others to use that knowledge; how can you exploit that coaching in order to win your particular game? The premise is simple: if you recognize the game in which you are playing for what it is – a common human experience – it will immediately become an easier game to play.

In April and May 1999 we were discussing a series of events that were current at the time and they all seemed to confirm the theory of games to which our research was pointing. The events were across domains and included Manchester United's chase for the treble, NATO's involvement in Kosovo, Microsoft's litigation, BMW's negotiations over Longbridge, Cronenberg's new film *eXistenZ*, the devolution elections, the Marks & Spencer crisis and BSkyB's attempted acquisition of Manchester United. Everywhere we looked we saw the MORES and players who had either understood or misunderstood them. We decided that an exploration and explanation of the gaming instinct would be a valuable exercise and that if we were right we could apply the model across domains. We therefore consolidated our model so that it provided a methodology for diagnosing and designing business games that was simple, comprehensive and robust. Each of the MORES has been sub-divided into easily identifiable segments and each segment sub-divided to its basic analytical unit. This means that readers can focus on issues to the depth they feel is appropriate. The model allows you, the reader, to apply it to your game and gain some insights. The book is intended to provide you with a series of pertinent questions to ask about the games you play – answering them will provide a competitive edge. So read on and tell us if we were right.

the idea

Humans are, by nature, game players and the business world is no more nor less than a series of games. It is, therefore, those players whose gaming instinct is most finely tuned who will play the game most successfully. The key differentiator of performance in any game will be the decision making of the players.

Powerful multinationals that compete with smaller and perhaps even more efficient organizations tend to be successful simply as a consequence of resource imbalance, rather than the quality of their decisions. So too with great war machines pitted against inferior forces. It was not decision making that provided the competitive advantage in the Second World War but the overwhelming resource base of the allies, particularly the United States. However, and this is where the significance of games is revealed, resource superiority did not win the Vietnam War and will not decide the ultimate outcome of Kosovo's problems. Vietnam, in particular, showed what happens when teams are competing against each other but playing different games. In cases where there is such a perceptual clash it is the team that best understands the actual game in which it is involved, or that can impose its version of the game on to the others, who will prevail.

In 1869 the first American football match was played by Rutgers University and Princeton University. Prior to the match both universities had established slightly different rules for the game they played. Rutgers was not permitted to catch or throw the ball, Princeton was. When using Rutgers' rules Rutgers won 6–4; when using Princeton's rules Princeton won 8–0. The competitive advantage went to the players with the deepest knowledge of the intricacies of the game. The players who had first-hand experience of the rules, structure and strategies of their own games were the most successful. The same is true in business. It is not enough simply to know which business you are in, you must also understand the deeper complexities of that game. If factors other than decision making, such as resources, are of sufficient weight they *can* become the dominant indicator of success in a chosen game. But where such factors are more or less equal, then superior decision-making skills will be the key success differentiator, the key competitive advantage.

why games?

why are games important?

There is only one thing more important than winning the game and that is maintaining the game.

What evidence is there that humans are the game players? There is a wealth of psychological literature and common-sense observation that tells us that human beings love to make life more complex than it needs to be. Human beings enjoy overcoming obstacles to such an extent that they actually create them. Animals do not do that. We have all seen squirrels overcoming enormously complex and difficult obstacles in their quest for the food placed there by humans. Who has ever seen the squirrel find some food and then construct obstacles in the way of eating it? Humans are different. They play with a ball and then decide to compete for it, to make a goal, a basket, a hole, a net, in order to make the competition even more difficult. Human beings play chess, draughts, Monopoly, poker and football – in fact, anything to test themselves.

Richard Dreyfuss, the star of *Jaws* and *Close Encounters*, explained the depression in his career and life in terms of this need:

I had won an Oscar, I was on top. And because that smooth path was not what I wanted I think I created a series of obstacles in my life. I need to overcome things, and having achieved success I said, 'Well, let's overcome drug addiction and stupidity and arrogance and bad movie picking!'

Animals find survival more than enough of a challenge to keep them occupied without adding to their difficulties by playing games. This is not to argue that animals do not play, but only in the sense of 'playfulness', rather than the structured interactions in which humans engage. Ironically our ability to erect these game structures means that in certain instances our decision making is inferior to that of lower animals. Psychological research has shown, for example, that while humans are vulnerable to the sunk-cost effect or Concorde fallacy, lower animals are not. (The 'Concorde fallacy' is so called because the Anglo-French airplane was financed even after it became obvious that by any economic calculations it should have been scrapped.)

This sunk-cost effect is apparent across many domains. In sport, for example, a 1995 study of the NBA (National Basketball Association) showed that the higher the draft pick, and consequently the higher the cost, the more playing time a player would be given. This enhanced playing time was given irrespective of the player's performance. Similarly, data from more than a thousand firms showed that those people who started their own businesses were much more likely to expand the business than those who bought the business as going concerns. An even more outrageous manifestation of the sunk-cost effect is that the expansions were more likely when the businesses began to fail.

The sunk-cost syndrome is similar to what psychologists Peter Ayton and Hal Arkes (1998) refer to as the 'prospect theory'. This theory suggests that 'people are more motivated by their losses than their gains, and this results in increasingly risky behaviour as the losses accumulate'. In the gambling fraternity it is called 'chasing your money' – the idea that the only way to recover losses is by seeking ever longer odds bets. High profile business examples abound. Nick Leeson at Barings, Yasuo Hamanaka at Sumitomo, an unnamed low-level employee at Electrolux and the less famous Hugh Eaves at Phillips & Drew (P&D), the fund management group, are just four. Their antics, and others like them, are now so prevalent that there is even a generic term for them – they are called 'rogue traders'. The least famous, the P&D case, has, perhaps, the most to teach the game analyst. The 'rogue trader' in this instance was a 56-year-old finance director by the name of Hugh Eaves. In 1985 the Union Bank of Switzerland (UBS) bought P&D and the partners of P&D received their payment in the form of equity in UBS. The partners then created a fund to manage the equities and entrusted Hugh Eaves with running the fund. Eaves was also a director of Bury Football Club and enjoyed the celebrity of being a high-profile football magnate. He invested millions in his home-town club. He was also known as a gambler and a comment by a source close to P&D perfectly encapsulates the sunk-cost dilemma (*Sunday Times*, 9 May 1999). The source said:

What appears to have happened is that Eaves used the equity in UBS as collateral and started trading. He ended up in a position where he had a tiger by the tail and tried to correct his errors. But instead of correcting them, he compounded them.

Why do people like Eaves and Leeson take such risks? The explanation might just be biological. Research (Odean) suggests that the level of an enzyme (MAO) found in human blood directly correlates to levels of risk taking. In general, risk taking is greater among the young than the old and among men than women. For the game player, information about the risk-taking propensity of others in the game is invaluable. Had the partners at P&D, for example, paid more attention to the 'laddish' alter-ego of their sober-suited colleague they might have been less inclined to trust him with their collective £20 million. Indeed, had they read the research of Professor Odean into trading results based on gender factors they may have been inclined to give their money to a woman. The Professor's research shows that women outperform their 'thrill-seeking' male counterparts, on a risk adjusted basis, by statistically significant amounts.

information about the risk-taking of others in the game is invaluable

What the research in this field also shows is that the intellectual capacity of humans to be able to create abstract rules, and by implication game structures, also leads to the possibility that those rules can be over-generalized, which in turn causes such phenomena as the Concorde fallacy. Combine this with the biological tendencies towards risk taking and you have the classic ingredients of the game player, only the mix is different.

Other psychological research also confirms the concept of a human predisposition towards gaming activities. Eric Berne, the eminent psychologist, called his book on the psychology of human relationships *Games People Play* (1964). In this work Berne argues that all the evidence of psychological research points to the fact that 'any social intercourse whatever has a biological advantage over no intercourse at all'. In other words, humans are social beings. He further contends that as a consequence of the human desire to interact, series of unwritten rules and regulations are created in order to 'pattern' our social interactions. These patterns form the structure of the game. Because Berne looks very specifically at individuals' relationships, his findings are especially useful to the business player, particularly when translated to an organizational context. Bernes emphasized the centrality of games for human existence – playing games is a basic instinct. Berne also makes the crucial point that we should not be misled by the use of the term 'game'. There is no implication in either Berne's usage, or ours, of the notion of 'fun'. Game playing is serious at any level.

alternative realities

Possibly the most significant factor in decision analysis is perception. Individuals and groups construct alternative realities for themselves and others and make decisions within those realities. They define the situation in which they find themselves and only then make the decision. It is the variety of realities created by individuals – and groups – that we are designating as games.

By concentrating on alternative realities we differ from some other theorists who write about games as a method of explaining organizational transactions – economists and mathematicians, for example. Economic 'game theorists' argue that in 'strategic games', that is to say those in which players have a choice of action and in which their actions are interdependent, it is possible to provide an optimal solution concerning the degree of co-operation or competition necessary to succeed (whilst allowing for the elements of imperfect information and chance that are clearly present in all games of this nature). However, there must be rationality and finite variables in order to make the calculations feasible. The inapplicability of such a theory of games was evident in its origins. It originated as a mathematical model that derived from the originator's fascination with poker. At the outset he was forced, by the sheer complexity of poker, to restrict the number of players to two, the bets to two, to disallow a draw and to have the cards face down. Although this formulation of the game retained the essential elements of the game it stripped away the crucial influence of virtually infinite variety (*see* Ashby, 1956, for an explanation of the significance of variety in organizational situations). As a consequence, despite the intellectual brilliance of the seminal work in game theory, it offers little help to the practising business player – with the possible exception of derivatives trading and 'risk technology'. Even in those areas it is more the exception than the rule. You cannot model games precisely because of their infinite variety.

Game theory can be effective as a diagnostic tool (*see* Nalebuff, 1996). However, it fails in practice. In early 1993, for example, the US Federal Communications Commission used academic game theoreticians (*see* McDonald, 1950) to design the auction bidding process for the sales of thousands of telecommunications spectrum licences worth in excess of $7 billion. It became necessary, for that brief period, for potential bidders to hire their own game theorists in order to develop the most rational bidding strategy that followed the rules of game theory. Whilst there was no evidence that the use of game theory affected the outcomes, which might have been predicted for any other auction process, what did emerge was that bidders actually circumvented the rules established by the auction designers. One telecoms operator, for example, highlighted his interest in specific licences by the simple mechanism of ending his bids with the zip code of the city in which he was interested. This, and other undetected subterfuges, effectively undermined the auction design and demonstrated the real art of game playing. In its present state game theory cannot provide the answers to the most interesting questions. In failing to account for different realities, game theoretic analyses are inevitably limited.

decision making

So far we have identified two crucial factors in decision making – first, a recognition of the underlying gaming structure of human interaction and second, the alternative realities constructed by those who play the games. But why do we place such importance on decision making? Because it is invariably the difference between success and failure and also because it has received insuffi-

decision making is invariably the difference between success and failure

cient attention as a differentiator. Jerre L. Stead, the chairman and CEO of one of the world's leading wholesale distributors of technology products and services, Ingram Micro Inc., puts it this way:

Sales people sell, administrators organize and engineers create, but executives decide. We decide to recruit new talent, open or close facilities, enter new lines of business or leave old ones. Through our decisions we influence other people's lives and spend other people's money. Our decisions determine our companies' fortunes. They also get us lionized and demonized. So, if our decisions carry so much weight, why don't we make it easier on ourselves to make better decisions? Effective decision making is rare in the corporate world, even though most companies contain the necessary elements.

When Stead talks about being 'lionized' or 'demonized' he gets to the heart of the decision-making dilemma: decisions have consequences and only after decisions have been taken can their effectiveness be measured. However, it is still necessary to develop a model for more effective decision making, and that can only be done by isolating the key variables in the process. If we assume that decision making is a skill within the structure of the game we have chosen to play, then we need to be aware of the variety of levels at which decision making occurs. These are the *strategic*, the *tactical*, the *operational* and the *crisis* levels. Strategic can be equated to policy, tactical to the chosen method of implementing that policy, and operational to the practical manifestation of the tactics. Crisis decision-making is the antithesis of good decision making but must also be seen as a necessary skill in the decision-making tool box.

There is also a recursive quality to the levels: the level of decision making is issue-dependent. In a major football club such as Manchester United, it is easy to see the levels of recursion. Viewed as a company then clearly it would be Martin Edwards making the strategic decisions, Alex Ferguson the tactical and Roy Keane the operational. However, if we focus on the first team only, then Ferguson is the strategist, with the coaches becoming the tacticians. Looking at the whole Manchester United football empire, including reserves, youth teams, academies and scouting system, it is obvious that all three decision-making levels are constantly engaged and dynamic. Within the context of the youth team, for example, the team's manager will make strategic decisions, but only within the parameters of the game plan established by the club manager. The youth team manager is the controller of that particular sub-system. The youth team manager's objective is not merely to win the youth league, but more importantly to produce players for the first team. Also, if the senior manager designates a particular system of play that he wishes to be followed throughout the club then that too will limit the possibilities for strategic decision making at the lower level. Nevertheless, even allowing for such constraints, the youth team manager has more scope to practise strategic decision making than *his* coach.

Decision making does not necessarily become strategic, tactical or operational merely in relation to its hierarchical location. This is even more the case with crisis decision making, which axiomatically occurs in an unplanned and chaotic manner anywhere in the organization. The recursive nature of the decision-making levels is shown in Table 1.1 and can be translated to any organization.

Table 1.1 Decision-making levels

	Group	Company	Function	Section	C
					R
					I
Strategic	Group CEO	Company CEO	Function head	Section head	S
Tactical	Company CEO	Function head	Section head	Section employees	I
Operational	Function head	Section head	Section employees	Operators	S

using analogies

Having established the significance of games in human experience, we must also distinguish our approach from others who use metaphors to explain business practices. Principally we differ in that we do not differentiate between business and others types of game. The business community has spent a good deal of time and energy trying to develop a single, precise analogy that explains business. War, sport, games (including board games and card games) and the creative industries (theatre companies, orchestras) are variously extolled for their analogous power. The problem with such attempts is that they are inevitably partial, because they seek to map perfectly one environment on to another. The mistake is that business is not *wholly* like any game, war or orchestra but is *very* like all of them, dependent on the specific situation.

It is because we view activities across domains as having identical underlying structures that we needed a generic term that would link any of them and business. The most appropriate generic term is 'game'. We accept that its common-sense usage as well as it economic and psychological usages may confuse, but it is this very breadth of usage that makes the term so apposite. For the purposes of this book we define a game as: 'any rule-bound interaction in which individuals or groups seek to achieve jointly recognized objectives'. In this context the term 'rule' includes 'codified' rules and 'conventions'. Reference to the significance of stated and unstated, explicit and implicit, open and hidden, complementary and ulterior rule systems will be prevalent throughout the book and form a vital ingredient of the game players' skill set.

However, metaphors can be enlightening. When we analyze the business game skill set we draw examples and case studies from the most appropriate source. These tend to be from the traditional gaming domains of war, sport, politics and the creative sectors. The reason we use these domains is simple – they are accessible and interesting and we learn most easily from stories that include those qualities. The stories we will tell are stories of games, played well and badly. From those stories we will derive guidelines for game players, which in some guise means us all. What makes games interesting is the 'How would I have played it?' question. It is the ability to be able to answer that question accurately, before and during the game, which gives game players the competitive advantage.

> what makes games interesting is the 'How would I have played it?' question

games and reality

Finally, before we outline our model for playing the business game, we must address those who argue that business is not a game or even *like* a game. Such people tend to distinguish between a notion of objective reality and games, using comments like, 'It's not like that in the *real* world'. For business people this 'real world' is business, for politicians it is politics, for military people it is war and so on. Even if at the moment you read this book you might agree that such a separation is sensible, you certainly will not think so ten years from now. Why not? Because the real and the fantasy are merging. There is already a blurring of what constitutes games (fantasy) and reality.

Our version of the future may well be the first appearance of post-modernist analysis in a business book. The post-modernists' deconstruction of language and events enables a transparent understanding of the game in which the player is involved. Think for a moment about three essays by the French philosopher Jean Baudrillard concerning the Gulf War. They were entitled 'The Gulf War will not take place', 'The Gulf War: is it really taking place?' and 'The Gulf War did not take place'. The first was written a month or so before the allied offensive began on 15 January 1991, the second in February, when the offensive was at its height, and the third immediately after the cessation of hostilities. At first sight, Baudrillard would not appear to be the ideal candidate to undertake a reality audit for corporate players. In fact, Baudrillard argued that what happened in the Gulf may have been a tragic and horrific disaster, but that in itself did not constitute a war. A war needs two protagonists, engaged in combat – an adversarial encounter. What happened in the Gulf was not a fight but a mugging. The imbalance between the sides was such that it was an exercise in domination rather than war. What kind of war is it where one of the 'combatants' has more casualties during training than during combat? What kind of war has a casualty rate for one of the 'combatants' that is three times less than the expected attrition rate from road traffic accidents had they stayed at home?

Baudrillard's second point was that what we actually saw was a 'virtual' conflict that masqueraded as real. The presentation of the 'war' for the public consumption effectively usurped the concept of reality for the television viewers. The absurdity of the first live television 'war' became obvious from the moment a CNN reporter linked live to other reporters on the ground in the Gulf. To his embarrassment, and probably theirs, they had to admit that they were watching CNN themselves in order to find out what was happening. At that same time, one of the authors of this book was working in the intelligence cell of the joint HQ in the United Kingdom. When friends and family asked for inside information they never believed his reply that CNN or the daily newspapers were pretty well accurate. There exists a simultaneous belief in the 'real' TV footage and some other 'real' that only those intimately involved know about. Interestingly, those who *are* intimately involved also subscribe to the same contradictory beliefs, presumably in the subconscious attempt to elevate their own importance.

post-modernist analysis uncovers the alternative realities of participants and reveals the structure of the game actually being played

What post-modernist analysis does at its best is to question reality and the nature of events. It uncovers the alternative realities of participants and as a consequence reveals the structure of the game actually being played. Surely such knowledge is a pre-requisite for effective game-playing. The transparency that post-modern analysis generates is a vital ingredient of strategic planning. All CEOs should have post-modernist consultants on their staff. They may not be able to identify which game the CEO wishes to play, but they can at least reveal the one that *is* being played and the alternatives available. It is not only in a philosophical sense that the boundaries between reality and games are blurring. It is happening in daily life. The disturbing evidence surfacing from the investigation into the carnage at Columbine High in Littleton, Colorado, caused many to register their concern at the over-spill from games to reality. The phenomenon is entirely predictable, given the basic gaming instinct. The Littleton killers were avid fans of the 3-D gore-fest game called 'Doom'. The ever-increasing power available to these games allows their virtual environment to generate 'real' emotions and real adrenaline. It also appears to develop transferable skills. The genre is referred to as 'first-person shooter' gaming, which teaches the skill of efficient killing in an antiseptic manner. The natural tendency of amateurs, for example, is to continue shooting until the gun is empty – many shots, one kill. The professional, by contrast, tries to use one shot per kill, usually a head shot.

the boundaries between reality and games are blurring

In another US school shooting, the killer was a 14 year-old Doom fan who had never fired a real gun before. He managed to hit eight separate targets with eight shots, five killed and three wounded. He moved efficiently from one target to the next without any apparent emotion. This is precisely what a seasoned professional would have done and it is precisely the requisite strategy for Doom players. A military expert on the US news programme, *60 Minutes*, called games like Doom a 'how-to manual for killing without conscience'. A specially adapted version of Doom has also been used to train US marines in virtual single-combat scenarios.

The inventor of Doom is John Romero. He refuses to discuss the ramifications of the Littleton massacre, possibly fearing for his own safety. Romero now has a fictional counterpart in David Cronenberg's 1999 film, *eXistenZ*. Cronenberg takes the phenomenon of 'virtuality' to its ultimate conclusion. In an otherwise forgettable film, he raises a fascinating spectre. In his world it is possible to plug gaming software directly into the nervous systems of individuals. This enables the 'player' to interact seamlessly with the game, thus virtual reality becomes reality and vice-versa. Another 1999 film to deal with this topic was the Keanu Reeves vehicle *The Matrix*, in which the distinction between reality and games is recognized but reversed. Cronenberg believes his film to be an allegory for a 'clash of realities'. He was inspired by the Salman Rushdie fatwa, which he argued was generated by the fact that 'Salman wrote his book out of the Western liberal tradition of freedom of expression and it was received by quite a different tradition in which that doesn't exist'. This lack of communication between realities, Cronenberg argues, is ultimately disastrous.

Such shifting and even switching of realities is a central theme of modern life. What else is spin-doctoring if not the manipulation of reality? Bernard Ingham, Margaret Thatcher's Press Officer for 11 years, accused the spin-doctors in just such terms: 'Spin-doctors are party apparatchiks who play games and are in the business of creating new realities' (*The Times*, 13 May 1999). A PricewaterhouseCoopers (PwC) publication on mergers and acquisitions also combines the concepts of game playing and reality. One of the central themes of the booklet (*Playing M & A poker with value as the chips*) is the ability of companies (players) 'to adapt to a new reality'.

The twin concepts of games and reality are clearly seen in educational business games. In 1998 and 1999 there was a 125-per-cent increase in attendance at the annual conference of the North American Simulation and Gaming Association (NASAGA). Board games such as 'Zodiak: the Game of Business Finance and Strategy' (http://www.paradigmlearning.com) and 'The Manufacturing Game' (http://www.mfg-game.com) are examples in which strategic and tactical skills are modelled in an attempt to create a simulated business environment. The Manufacturing Game was originally created by Dupont after an extensive three-year benchmarking exercise into the nature of world-class maintenance and relia-bility practices. The result of the benchmarking was a realization that the elements of their success were generic and could be incorporated into a board game that modelled the operations, business services and maintenance functions and used poker chips to represent the products, supplies and resources involved in the manufacturing process as a whole. Businesses such as BP have utilized the Manufacturing Game in their restructuring processes, especially as a method of inducing employee buy-in. As players are encouraged to adopt different roles from their actual role in the company, they can more readily appreciate the difficulties faced by their counterparts throughout the organization.

Electronic equivalents of these board games are also becoming available. 'Capitalism Plus', (http://www.imagicgames.com) for example, is a powerful example of electronic gaming which enables skills to be developed in the complex arena of mergers and acquisitions. Companies who use game simulation, either tradi-tional or electronic, implicitly accept our premise of business as just another gaming arena. Unfortunately, *e*xplicitly they reject it by their over reliance on game-as-simulation rather than game-as-model – a subtle but significant difference.

the game-playing model

This book is not only about the theory of a gaming instinct but also a practical account of how to hone the game playing process and then use it for competitive advantage. Imagine you are being forced to play a game of which you had no prior knowledge. What questions would you ask? Our research, across all domains, generated remarkably similar answers. At root there are just five questions. First, why am I playing, what is my *motive*? Second, who else is playing, who are my opponents and collaborators, the significant *others*? Third, what are the *rules*, what are the limits of the rules and consequences for breaking them? Fourth, what are the conditions, in what *environment* does this game operate? Fifth, what *skills* are needed for this game, have I got them, how can I acquire them? We have translated the answers into a simple mnemonic, MORES – **m**otivation, **o**thers, **r**ules, **e**nvironment, **s**kills. Interestingly, one definition of the word 'mores' is 'customs or conventions regarded as essential or vital to a social group'. This book provides a guide to the mores of the social group known as game players, and in our view that includes us all.

What then are the vital elements needed to turn this information into a winning formula? By the term 'winning' we mean players achieving their maximum potential in their chosen game. Clearly the criteria by which we judge such achievement will be different for an individual, a team, a limited company, a private company, a corner shop or a public enterprise. We identified three elements that provide the edge necessary for success. They are *knowledge*, *coaching* and *exploiting*. Without sufficient knowledge of each of the MORES, failure is inevitable. Coaching is the ability to be able to facilitate the application of knowledge by others – it is guided practice. Exploitation is how you actually play the game. In simple diagrammatic form the interrelationship of the varying components of the gaming situation is shown in Figure 1.1 (overleaf). The diagram shows that winning can only be achieved by developing an extensive knowledge of the elements of the game to be played, coaching the players relative to that knowledge and then exploiting the coaching and knowledge in the playing of the game itself. The remainder of the book is devoted to explaining each aspect of the game-playing process and how they relate to gaining a competitive advantage.

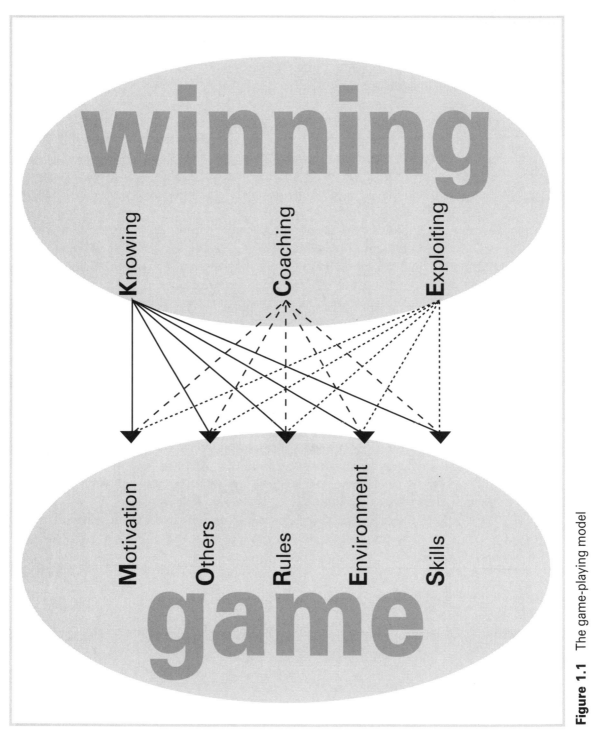

Figure 1.1 The game-playing model

the game

The vital ingredients of the game can be expressed by the mnemonic MORES, but the order of the components is merely to aid recollection and is in no way hierarchical. Indeed, each element is intimately inter-related with the others and they are only isolated in the text for ease of discussion. *Motivation* without *skill*, for example, is the definition of an amateur. A lack of awareness of the abilities and needs of the *others* in the game is a recipe for defeat, as is an inadequate knowledge of the *rules*. Finally, the *environment* in which the game takes place affects each of the other factors. As a consequence of the interconnection of all five factors, winning any game will involve understanding the significance and interrelationships of them all. Therefore, while we treat each element separately we are careful to identify where they overlap and we also urge readers to make connections from their own experience as they recognize them.

motivation

why do we play?

Everybody has the will to win; only the very best have the will to prepare to win.

Despite the mountains of literature that organizational theorists have expended on the subject of *motivation*, essentially it is about two questions – why do players play and why do players play the way they do? Organizational theorists have defined these stages as *why* people work and *how* people work.

why we play

There is a close correlation between an organization's desire to continue to exist and an individual's desire to work, since neither are ultimately necessary to the survival of either entity. An early survey conducted on a Bristol workforce found that 69 per cent of men interviewed, and 65 per cent of women, would choose to continue to work even if there were no financial necessity to do so. This finding fits precisely with our view of work as simply another form of game in which humans have some need to engage. So why then do players choose particular games, or why do workers choose particular jobs? In other words, why do players play?

Modern business theories are dismissive of Maslow's hierarchy of needs (1943) in which he argues that basic needs have to be satisfied in a sequential manner before the next higher level of needs become significant. However, the significance of Maslow's theory for game players is that it places equal emphasis on both gratification and deprivation as the crucial concepts of motivation theory. Critics of Maslow, and to a certain extent of Herzberg's two factor theory (1968), argue that there is a little empirical evidence to support either the notion of sequential satisfaction or, indeed, that Maslow's five levels are even distinguishable as categories. While the terms can certainly be criticized or even redefined, they are essentially accurate in that they clearly refer to internally generated criteria for the strength and direction of human behaviour. It is difficult to disagree with Hertzberg's 'positive' motivation factors of achievement or his 'negative' factors such as salary and company policy. We are not interested in this book in knowing *why* such criteria are generated, only in accepting that they are and then assessing how that knowledge might be used to maximize success.

So, why *do* players play? Our research suggests that something akin to Maslow's hierarchy exists, but that the levels are most closely correlated to socio-economic status. At the lowest socio-economic only *survival* is important. How the individual, family or group survives from day to day is their primary concern. The same explanation can be applied to start-up businesses. Start-ups need to address themselves to survival in that first crucial year in which a majority of new businesses are known to fail. Thoughts of profit, expansion and comfort are

how the individual, family or group survives from day to day is their primary concern

irrelevant at the initial stage of development, where only continued existence counts.

Satisfaction at this level allows the individual or business to begin to attempt to stabilize and protect themselves. In the *stability* phase the business has survived the first dangerous period and needs to erect a defence system against threats that will deprive it of its hard-won identity. It must secure its supply and maintenance lines, protect its cash flow and minimize any capital depreciation. Having consolidated this defence system the organization or individual can begin to explore alternative routes towards the satisfaction of the 'higher' need – *comfort*. Of course, the definition of what each organization perceives as filling these criteria will be particular to that organization. Equally, what will appear possible relies heavily on the exposure to the alternatives that the members of the organisation have received. Horizons *can* be raised but only if there is an awareness that such an act is possible. We can only do what we can imagine. When Bill Gates said he wanted a PC 'on every desk and in every home' perhaps his imagination had translated Coca-Cola bottles into PCs so that the omnipresence of Coca-Cola became Gates's model.

As Maslow said, however, once a need has been satisfied then the organism will seek to satisfy another 'higher' need. These new needs may be described in terms of market position – for example, how do we become 'number one'? If that is not possible, then the question might be, what *can* we achieve, what is our potential? Do the limitations of our organization preclude us from competing with the very best? Is it possible, for example, for a newly constituted car manufacturer to challenge the dominance of Ford or GM? Is it possible for Safeway to cut significantly into the market share of Tesco or Sainsbury's? None of these scenarios seems remotely likely and yet the organizations do not simply fade away. They may have reached their motivational equilibrium and be content to maintain and very gradually improve their position. Their motivation is to stay in the game not necessarily to win it – that becomes *their* victory. Similarly, for Safeway the maintenance of its market share in the face of the super battalions of Wal-Mart, Asda and Tesco would satisfy its self-perceptions of fulfilment.

Organizations benchmark themselves against others just as we do as human beings. We recognize role models – people who have achieved what we would like to achieve. When we have emulated or even supplanted our role models we, in our turn, become the role models for someone else. Our new goal becomes the maintenance of our new position and even search for other, higher targets. Where do you go when you have won the treble? This was a rhetorical question posed to Manchester United at the end of the 1998–9 season. Their target subsequently became to establish new markers in the same way that Tim Redgrave covets a fifth Olympics and Bill Gates stays in business despite his multi-billionaire status. What has happened to them all is an assimilation into a particular reality (a game). In that zone the motivation to be involved is not even questioned. In this book we refer to such immersion as 'socialization'. Once socialization has occurred then the higher zones of *expansion* and *supremacy* can be pursued. The motivation at these higher levels is driven by the innate human need to be challenged and judged.

For Maslow the highest human need, 'self-actualization', was actually what might best be described as 'fitted-ness' – the notion that a musician must make music, that the creative must create. While most people are not in the job most suited to them, they are still motivated to succeed. They are still sufficiently socialized in the game to establish their own criteria of success – even if they quietly pine to be the artist, musician or footballer of their dreams. Despite the virtually never-ending academic debate surrounding motivational theories we argue that for practical purposes there *is* a hierarchy. This hierarchy – for both individuals and organizations – is sequential and overlapping: remnants of different levels remain in the psyche and continue to affect participation in the game (*see* Fig. 2.1).

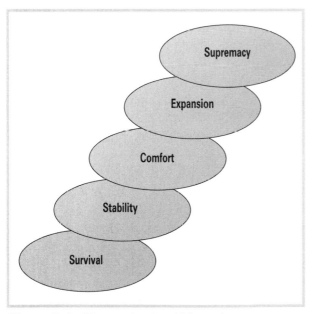

Figure 2.1 The motivational hierarchy

The story of one of our interviewees perhaps illustrates this motivational process most clearly. Bill Stealey is the CEO of Interactive Magic, a software gaming firm with a massive annual turnover. He has a personal fortune of $24 million. We asked 'Wild Bill', as he is called, what motivated him to get into business. He responded immediately:

My Dad died when I was eight and we were poor. I thought, let's not be poor. I joined the US Air Force but didn't really fit into a peacetime force, so I left. I went to Wharton to be the General in business that I couldn't be in the Air Force. I wanted to be a business General because I thought I would be good at it. I was. I suppose my motivation was poverty and ego.

Having achieved his comfort zone, Bill Stealey owned an indoor football (soccer) team, the Baltimore Spirit, for a period of six years from 1991 to 1997. They lost money every year. 'Would you have continued had it been any other business than football?' we asked Stealey. 'Of course not', he replied. 'Then why did you go on?' 'Because it's football.' Ron Noades, the owner/manager of Brentford FC gave precisely the same answer. We asked Ron the following question: 'On the radio recently you said that if you wanted to make money then don't go into football. So why did you do it?' 'It's football,' he replied.

> once the basic needs have been satisfied then other needs will be pursued and satisfied

What these examples demonstrate is that once the basic needs have been satisfied then other needs will be pursued and satisfied. Both Stealey and Noades were secure enough to engage in games that gave them greater personal fulfilment. It is clear that self-fulfilment is individually defined. So how can players *in* the game be motivated to improve their performance?

why players play the way they do

Phrases like 'the team was highly motivated', or 'the team was demotivated', or 'the coach must motivate them', or a player 'lacks motivation' are all comments about performance. Why is it that talented players fail to produce talented performances? Why do some workers give up when others keep going? Why are some people constantly absent while others never lose a day? Why do some consistently achieve high productivity and others consistently underachieve? Those responsible for performance are not interested in *why* someone plays, only in *how* they play. This is one of the reasons that organizational behaviourists have been so active in this field. They argue that because notions such as motivation and satisfaction are only hypothetical constructs, then only actual behaviour is worth observing because that is what you are trying to change. They do not seek to explain behaviour, but to alter it. For the behaviourist this is not as manipulative as it might sound, since they contend that all behaviour is learned (countering arguments of human innateness). They believe that behaviour is altered most effectively (learned) in relation to the consequences that occur immediately after an event. These consequences are sub-divided into four categories – *positive reinforcement, negative reinforcement, punishment* and *neglect.*

Table 2.1 Altering behaviour

Consequence	Effect
Positive reinforcement	Increase
Negative reinforcement	Increase
Punishment	Decrease
Neglect	Decrease

Behaviourists contend that the result of each category is either to increase or decrease the relevant behaviour, as shown in Table 2.1. In the business game we would want to encourage (increase) productive behaviour and discourage (decrease) unproductive behaviour. Reinforcement, either positive or negative, will increase the likelihood of behaviour being repeated. Positive reinforcement is defined as something the recipient will perceive as a reward. That the recipient perceives the consequence as a reward is crucial. For example, whether to increase overtime payments or give more time off is a common dilemma for management seeking to reward the workforce. It is a dilemma because within any group there will be a split as to which option is perceived as the greatest reward.

Negative reinforcement increases the frequency of targeted behaviour by removing unpleasant stimuli. The ludicrous policy of logging toilet breaks in some major call-centres would be a typically unpleasant stimulus. Removing it would, therefore, be viewed in the same light as a reward. Punishment and neglect will both decrease behaviour in a somewhat Pavlovian sense.

For the behaviourist, therefore, behavioural change is a mechanistic affair:

- identify behaviour to be altered
- measure its frequency
- develop an intervention strategy
- implement it
- measure the effects of the strategy
- repeat the cycle if necessary.

If it is so easy, why aren't all workforces subjected to this process? Because it is not that easy! An oft-cited piece of research by Brand *et al.* (1982) illustrates the difficulty of attaching complete significance to observation-behaviourist methods. In the 1980s Brand and others conducted an organizational project that concentrated on the identification of critical behaviour, the establishment of individual performance indicators, transparent feedback and non-financial rewards for increased frequency of desired behaviours. The results showed an 800-per-cent increase in productivity and an increase in accuracy from 82 per cent to 99 per cent. However, one employee was singled out by the researchers for special mention because he was found to be contributing 20 per cent of the workload for a 12-man group and had an accuracy rating of 99.8 per cent. He explained that until this project no one had ever mentioned his performance. This was cited by the authors as evidence of a poor managerial attitude, which it clearly was; and yet this employee had performed almost perfectly for 17 years. Why? Because he wanted to. He derived some internal satisfaction from his work.

The real value of motivational theories to organizations is their suggestion that such internally generated behaviour exists. Such knowledge allows the behaviourist model to be employed effectively. This is where those who advocate variants of expectancy–valence theory (Steers and Porter, 1979) can complement behaviourist theories: not by attempting a general theory of motivation but by developing individually based motivational techniques. Like most nature–nurture debates the truth lies somewhere between the two extremes. Motivational drivers are most likely to be a combination of external (behaviourist) and internal (individualist) forces on the individual or organization. What this means for management is a need to recognize that goal-setting and job design cannot sensibly be imposed on a workforce without reference to the expectancies contained within the force. There is nothing more *de*motivating than unrealized expectations, irrespective as to how unrealistic they might have been. Goal

goals must be established as the result of consultations between management and staff

setting has beneficial effects on performance, but the goals must be established as the result of consultations between management and staff. The failure of performance indicators in many public services during the 1990s was a direct consequence of management's reluctance or inability to engage in such consultation. Management needs to set in place mechanisms for:

● revealing individual and group expectations and perceptions of valued rewards;

● ensuring that those expectations are realistic;

● ensuring an observable link between performance and reward;

● ensuring equity;

● ensuring that expectations within the organization do not conflict.

A central plank of the behaviourist methodology is the utility of behavioural measurement. Whilst we agree that it is not possible to measure motivation, it *can* be felt or intuited by management with sensitive antennae. This is why internal intelligence gathering is so crucial. Management must establish a free and transparent flow of information around the organization and it must actively develop a monitoring system that will be sensitive to mood swings in the organization. Such a monitoring function should access the information at predictable choke points, for example the water-cooler or coffee shop. If these areas do not exist, then create them. More importantly, give greater weight to data gleaned from these sources rather than from any formal questionnaires.

What about that group of people we might designate as obsessives: those whom we recognize as being driven? As well as the compulsive gamblers, like Hugh Eaves, and those who get behind the curve chasing money, like Nick Leeson, there is another group: the Margaret Thatchers, Rupert Murdochs and Bill Gates of this world. In fact, probably every CEO in the FTSE top 500. Again, the source of their obsession is irrelevant, except in that it is a key factor in their performance. But it is essential for any game-player to know how an opponent or ally is motivated and precisely what drivers are likely to affect their performance. Are they obsessives, like Thatcher, for whom a comfort zone was an anathema? Are they driven by fear of returning to the survival zone, like the ghetto-bred boxer Roberto Duran must have been? Are they gamblers? Have they an inner serenity that means they are happy with their lot? Have they the barely repressed violence of a Mike Tyson, or the self-imposed, introspective discipline of a Geoff Boycott? Are they motivated by self judgement or by a need for the approbation and respect of others?

The example of Roberto Duran demonstrates one of the ways in which knowledge of motivation may be used by other players against an individual. Not only was Duran obviously motivated by a desire to escape the ghetto, but he was also motivated by the culture of Latin machismo that was so central to his upbringing. It was said that Duran's nemesis, Sugar Ray Leonard, targeted this facet of the Duran personality in their great fights. Arguably Duran never recovered mentally from his ignominious surrender. By undermining an individual's or organization's strength you destroy the core of their being. Maslow (1943) said that when we delve into individuals' motivation 'we deal with [their] very essence'. So the answers to the questions of motivation are vital pieces of information for the game player. Managers must seek the answers from the players themselves (the workforce) because if nothing else is certain about motivation it is that externally imposed motivators have, at best, short-term benefits and are, at worst, destructive forces.

A recent addition to management literature by two Stanford academics (Pfeffer and Sutton, 1999) makes this precise point. They cite the fear-merchants of the early 1990s, Al Dunlap and Andy Grove, as classic examples of the short-termism of such methods. Dunlap was the down-sizing king and earned himself the nickname of 'Chainsaw Al'. Live by the chainsaw, die by the chainsaw. Dunlap was himself downsized after his methods backfired miserably during his two-year leadership of Sunbeam, during which time the company's fortunes dipped dramatically.

Andy Grove's methods at Intel have led to what must be one of the earliest manifestations of an 'e-union', with employees posting grievances on the company website. We believe that Grove was probably correct in saying that the 'role of mangers is to create an environment in which people are passionately dedicated to winning'. However, we disagree with him that 'fear plays a major role in creating and maintaining such passion'. There is a role for fear, but it is the same as every other motivational factor – it will only work in the long term if it is developed and implemented in a player-sensitive manner. Great corporate players need to understand what motivates themselves, their staff and their opponents and make plans that best utilize that knowledge.

others

who else is playing?

Differentiate between competitors, collaborators and complementors and then play *them* – with skill.

Who are the players in the business game? Once you begin to think of game playing in the generic sense, then virtually everyone has a role to play. It is also clear that new players actually change the game by their presence. A common mistake in business is to analyze the impact of new players without recognizing that the game will have changed with that new player's arrival.

Strategic planners are especially weak when the new player is their own organization. They fail to account for the changes in the game that their organization's presence will generate. As a consequence they develop game plans (strategies) based on the game as it was and not as it has become. Cable & Wireless (C&W) for example, spotted an opportunity to enter the business and domestic telecommunications market in the UK. They did not envisage the massive expansion in domestic demand for cable facilities which was, at least in part, generated by the appearance of a global player like C&W. They were forced to reassess, or more accurately reaffirm their commitment to business users and offload the domestic elements to NTL. The identification of significant players in any game is crucial to being able to play that game effectively. These players are not only competitors, because just as there is no such thing as the perfect market, so too is there no such thing as the perfect competition. Recognizing this fact is merely recognizing that games cannot be played in chaos. Even in the purest combat – boxing – the role of the trainers, managers, cornermen, crowd, referee and judges can, especially in close contests, prove to be the most important factor.

We need judges because we want to be completely immersed in the actual playing of the game and to be unencumbered by the trivialities of monitoring it. Everybody wants to play, but they recognize that to do so effectively they really need adjudicators. So as we come to identify the others in the game we are best advised to do so by role. How do players perceive themselves and how are they perceived by others? Are they, for example, competitors or adjudicators or some other type of player? What the games analyst must do is clearly define these roles and the effect they have upon the outcome of the game. It is difficult, not least because the relative importance of the roles appears to be fluid. In some games, for example, referees are virtually invisible, whereas in others they are the primary influence on the result. In orchestras those who collaborate with you are more important than those who compete. In the business world the role of the regulator has become a far more significant factor in the post-privatization period than it ever was before.

The other players in the corporate game can best be described as a 'co-opetive' mix'. The term is derived from 'co-opetition', first used by Ray Noorda, the founder of the Novell software company, and later developed by Nalebuff and Brandenburger (1996). According to Noorda, co-opetition is the natural state of business in which 'you have to compete and co-operate at the same time'. In this book then, the co-opetive-mix is the optimum combination of competitive and co-operative contributions by the significant game players. The mix is significant both within an organization and between organizations. A keen awareness and responsiveness to the co-opetive mix is essential to successful game playing. In simple terms, players need to know who contributes what,

players need to know who contributes what, and how they contribute it

and how they contribute it. Moreover, in no game can pure competition ever be the sole imperative. Such a policy would inevitably destroy the game. Since we believe that once players are 'socialized' into the game they will seek to maintain it, a level of co-operation must be essential to the well-being of the game. Companies need to know that *their* game is safe before committing the resources necessary to play it. As the time approaches for the renewal of rail contracts, for example, we see companies unwilling to invest because they are unsure of the continued existence of the game. Soon they will need to bond together in order to negotiate with the games inventors and administrators – the government.

To analyze the co-opetive mix, corporate players need to identify the sub-categories into which other players fall. We have identified six ingredients that contribute to the mix (*see* Fig. 3.1). Game players should use this guide to identify the functions others are performing in the game – and it is not always obvious. Competitive advantage is generated by a knowledge of both the players *and* their functions.

Figure 3.1 The co-opetive mix

owners

shareholders

Shareholders are the individuals or groups who own publicly quoted companies. Everything that is done by senior management is legally done in the name of their shareholders. Although shareholders have liability, it is limited, and the opposite side of the coin is potentially unlimited profit, either in relation to asset prices or increases in share price. Shareholders have ultimate power, although in practice that power is, or at least has been, under-utilized. Boards of directors have traditionally controlled the company and shareholders have been happy or unhappy with dividends and performance, but little more. This has also tended to be true of institutional investors, who typically employed a hands-off approach to operational issues. However, Thatcherism and Reaganomics led to a massive expansion in the equity markets and Thatcher's shareholding, house-owning population had a very simple expectation – to make money. That expectation was translated by the institutional investors, where individuals' money was located, into pressure on the companies. The companies responded to the actuarially led management of the institutional investor by focusing on shareholder value (SHV). A look at Fig. 3.2 shows the massive rise in ownership of organizations by institutional investors, a proportion that is now more than 80 per cent.

The influence of these institutions can also be exerted in a negative sense if the investors choose to transfer their funds. All pension funds, for example, have a portfolio of investments and judge each investment not in any absolute sense but

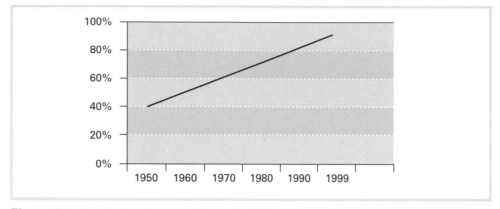

Figure 3.2 Institutional ownership in the UK

relative to the performance of the entire portfolio. Where they perceive weakened performance they will be tempted to either switch or pressurize the management. Companies can consequently find themselves paying out disproportionately high dividends in relation to after-tax profits. This process fuels the concentration on short-term investment portfolio performance in preference to corporate value. Advocates of SHV argue that the solution to this problem would be reforms of the UK's tax system (Black *et al.*, 1997). However, we think that systemic pressures will control short-termism and limit the worst excesses of SHV. Ironically, the strongest brake on short-termism might be applied by the largest institutional investors. Some of the US pension funds, for example, have portfolios that exceed $100 billion. They, like their British counterparts, have two legal obligations: they must benefit their members (maximize dividends) by prudent management of the funds.

This is where the systemic view is best appreciated. To operate most effectively a system must stay in equilibrium. If the equilibrium is compromised the system will begin to oscillate and eventually collapse. If any large institutional investor began moving $100 billion it would oscillate (disrupt) the market, which would clearly not be in the prudent interest of their members. Consequently, for these massive investors, intervention provides a more appropriate tactic than movement. The interventions can range from private meetings with the directors of under-performing companies to public denouncements. Once these super-investors register their dissatisfaction the management team is forced to respond. If it does not then the activist shareholders will remove it. So we return to the attempt to perfect the co-opetive mix – that cocktail of competing pressures. The argument against the stabilizing effects of the super-investors is the inherent

to operate most effectively a system must stay in equilibrium

volatility of the equity markets, which encourages short-termism. The market makes its judgements almost solely on cash flow and returns to shareholders. These simple criteria affect the fragile and mysterious confidence of the market. Trying to judge that confidence is yet another variable the business player must understand.

other ownership models

Shareholders do not represent the only ownership model. One model making something of a high-profile comeback is the co-operative. A large-scale example consists of the volunteer contributions made by open-source 'communities' of software developers who create software programmes for the Linux operating system. Linux, developed by 21-year-old Linus Torvalds in Finland in 1991, was a free and more robust alternative to commercial software such as Microsoft. Torvalds developed his idea on the launch, in 1984, of the Free Software Foundation, under whose auspices software was distributed free, providing that any developments made to the software were also passed on free. In a sense this movement was the perfect co-operative. However, like most successful co-operatives, this geeks' paradise is beginning to crack under the pressures of mammon. In August 1999 a company called Red Hat was floated. Red Hat shares tripled on its first day of trading. Red Hat supplies, at a cost, versions of Linux. Now volunteers want to know why shareholders will profit from their (the volunteers') efforts. Linux must manage this commercialization without alienating its source of competitive advantage – the volunteer geeks. If it fails to do so it will be competing directly with Microsoft without an edge and in that scenario there can be only one winner. Sadly this 'virtual' co-operative seems doomed to mimic most workers' co-operatives over time. Their lack of business drive generally proves fatal. This can be particularly evident in the 'touchy-feely' world of creative endeavour where equality of contribution is so highly valued. When the firm begins to succeed, egos and greed raise their ugly heads.

An extremely close relative of the co-operative model is the mutual company. A mutual company is one in which the organization is owned by the customers in recognition of their participation in that business. Ownership cannot be traded and is only conferred upon participants. A pamphlet published by the Co-operative Party is entitled *New Mutualism: a Golden Goal?* (Michie, 1999). In the foreword to the pamphlet the then Minister of Sport, Tony Banks, stated that 'many supporters had first-hand experience of the shortcomings of traditional forms of ownership [in football], where the club's future rests with one individual who may or may not pull out at any time'. He cites Brighton and Doncaster as near tragic examples. Conversely, Northampton Town and Bournemouth are the clubs that are consistently cited as examples of how mutualism can save a club. However, neither club is actually owned by their fans but rather each is partially owned by trusts.

Northampton Town Supporters' Trust, for example, owns 8 per cent of the shares. The Trust is chaired by Brian Lomax who was previously an editor of the fanzine.

Worldwide there are other notable examples of more genuinely mutual forms. These include the Green Bay Packers in the American NFL and the mighty Barcelona of Spain. The problem with both clubs is that their enormous membership base effectively distances senior management from any genuine membership control. In fact, Barcelona's president is seeking to move the club towards a more commercial status in order to compete with Manchester United's phenomenal financial power. The fans may

the very success of the mutual ventures may sound their death knell

prove powerless to resist such a commercial imperative. As with the co-operatives, the very success of the mutual ventures may sound their death knell, which has been the case with the building societies. A more effective tactic may be for fans to purchase shares. By subsequently forming blocks they may then have a genuine stake in their club and even force a seat on the board. Ajax of Amsterdam, for instance, has reserved the majority of its shares for its supporters.

Despite such attempts at community involvement, the future for business looks like more of the same; if anything, an even more ruthless interpretation of SHV may prevail. Mutualism may have come to the rescue of small clubs like Northampton but the Premier League clubs are still coveted by media and leisure giants. Even that paragon of co-operatism, the John Lewis Partnership, is beginning to hear stirrings from some of its 39,000 employees (the 'partners'). If the company were to be sold or floated it could expect to fetch close to £4 billion. Evenly divided, this would value the share of each 'partner' at £100,000. Despite the protestations of the chairman, Sir Stuart Hampson, that the partnership will never be sold during his tenure, it must be recognized that he has already more than £100,000. That sum may be more tempting to his employees than it is to him. All partnerships are subject to such pressures: The super-consultancy partnerships such as PricewaterhouseCoopers (PwC) and KPMG are already beginning to break up. The investigations of PwC by US regulators has forced it to separate out its management and auditing functions.

The traditional model, in football at least, which mutualism hopes to replace, is the local businessman model: the Cobbolds of Ipswich, the Moores of Liverpool, the Agnellis of Juventus, Berlusconi at Milan, Edwards at Manchester United. Other clubs with either an individual or a family as the majority shareholders include Arsenal, West Ham, Aston Villa, Everton, Derby, Middlesborough, Spurs, Newcastle, Wimbledon, Sunderland, and Bradford. These business players are owner-managers. The same phenomenon is present in business at large. Agnelli is also the patron of Fiat, Berlusconi has a communication empire, Rupert Murdoch has the News International Corporation and the Quandt family controls BMW. These business giants retain a controlling shareholding in the organizations they either founded or acquired. Their influence is omnipresent. Finally there are quasi-governmental bodies such as the European Commission. Who owns the commission, for example? Whether it is owned by its president or merely run by him, his significance as a player must be recognized.

managers

The next group of players are the managers. They actually run the organization for the benefit of those owners. These players are the appointed CEOs, the senior management team, the board and middle managers. This group must also include the Murdochs, Gates and Bransons of the world who, while they might choose to devolve some responsibility, nevertheless retain ultimate control. When we asked our old friend 'Wild Bill' Stealey of Interactive Magic how he apportioned duties between himself (the owner) and his CEO, he said, 'He does all the things I can't stand to do.'

Whatever the level of these managers, they are the players around whom discussions concerning leadership are centred. Leadership is a strange beast. It is difficult to analyze but even more difficult to develop or train. The key factor that links great leaders is their opportunism. They are able to spot and exploit opportunities. Obviously, communication skills, charisma, integrity and knowledge are important, but without the ability to seize opportunities they will be wasted. Since it is the owners who appoint the managers, it is they who must recognize, in their selections, the skills of the opportunist.

Those who appoint managers must also take into account a plethora of political factors. The appointment of the current head of BMW is a case in point. The boardroom battle between the previous head, Berndt Pischetsrieder, and his long-time colleague, Wolfgang Reitzle, was a battle between two dapper, flamboyant, stylish, opinionated and talented men. What both men misunderstood was the desire of the controlling Quandt family to preserve the BMW's image for stability. After the blood bath BMW needed tranquillity. From relative obscurity came Joachim Milberg, a quiet spoken academic. He was the appropriate choice for the most important aspect of the perceived tasks. So, when Reitzle was sacked by BMW – at least in part for his flamboyance, ruthlessness in cost-cutting and preference for elite products – he was hired by Ford for precisely the same qualities. Similar examples are obvious across the managerial spectrum. Graham Taylor's spectacular success with Watford but ignominious failure with England is one of the more clear-cut cases, but readers will be able to provide similar examples from their own domains.

It is, therefore, crucial to understand the significance of appropriateness and opportunism for managerial success. The final attribute to consider is enthusiasm. People being managed will forgive just about anything if the manager is an enthusiast. Without enthusiasm, any manager will eventually fail.

workers

The next category is the workforce – those who are managed and those who ultimately produce the product. While these players make up the majority in all games, in business they tend to receive the least attention, even though no organization can operate without them. The fact that the workforce has such latent power, and that mostly it remains latent, is an issue that periodically surfaces to embarrass and concern managers and owners alike. The good manager is sufficiently attuned to the workforce to sense discontent and manage it. However, if owners fail to understand the importance of workers then the manager may be hamstrung. Alex Ferguson, for example, very nearly lost the services of Roy Keane over pay demands that Martin Edwards was reluctant to meet. Despite the changes that occurred under Margaret Thatcher, the unions – as the voice of the workforce – must still be recognized as a major player. Both workers and management need to understand the power of the workforce: failure to do so by either party seriously disadvantages that party.

both workers and management need to understand the power of the workforce

How you deal with workforces will depend on how you view them and how they view themselves. There is, for example, something intrinsically different in dealing with a workforce like actors and sportsmen, who might perhaps work for nothing, and production-line workers, who are there merely to fund their 'real' existence. Between the two ends of the spectrum there are naturally gradations of workers for whom the job has a variety of motivational functions. For the manager, understanding where players lie on the spectrum, and where they aspire to lie on it, is a crucial advantage and one that calls for genuine investment of time. We argue that it is a worthwhile investment.

supporters

The term 'supporters' encompasses a whole raft of players, without whom the organization would sink. These are as diverse as *customers*, *suppliers*, *partners*, *stakeholders* and *complementors*. Customers and suppliers need little explanation, but some time has to be taken to define partners, stakeholders and complementors.

partners

Partners include external and internal others who enable the organization to survive and prosper. Internally, this is primarily the workforce, with whom sensible organizations form managerial partnerships. The TUC estimates that more than 50 companies have signed partnership agreements with trade unions. Again, it must be emphasized that these are not the confrontational agreements of old, but are genuine attempts to add to the company's competitive edge. Companies as diverse as BT, ICI, Prudential and BAe are in the vanguard of this approach. So too are non-union companies such as Asda and IBM. For the workforce, such partnerships can guarantee a commitment for employment security and the management should see value added through improved performance.

External partnerships between organizations are the stuff of many business books and include strategic partners, alliances, mergers and acquisitions. Let us look firstly at alliances. These are not necessarily – in fact not often – fixed. The dictum 'my enemy's enemy is my friend' is therefore a strong indicator when choosing allies. Allies are rarely a matter of simple choice – they are mostly unavoidable necessities.

A survey of the telecommunications industry is a case in point. Here the speed of the technological advances means that players have to pick and choose their allies swiftly and carefully. In the telecoms game the major players are already building networks to underpin their strategic imperatives. Once Bill Gates recognized the need to switch from focusing on PCs to focusing on the Internet and its accompanying services and devices, the alliance die was cast. He needed access to the vehicles for delivering the services. Hence, in May 1999, Microsoft took a $5 billion stake in AT&T. Why? Because AT&T had just bought TCI, one of the largest cable companies in the US, a part of John Malone's Liberty Media empire. This acquisition gained AT&T access to the local markets. Its chairman, Michael Armstrong, believed it was the natural expansion area. What TCI brought to the alliance was immediate access to more than 10 million homes that were already hooked up to TCI. Malone's Liberty Media operates as an autonomous unit, despite being a wholly owned subsidiary of AT&T. As an autonomous unit, Malone purchased an 8-per-cent stake in Rupert Murdoch's News Corporation – which of course, gives access to BSkyB. This, added to his stakes in Telewest, Britain's second largest cable company, and Flextech, make Malone a major player, although *the* player remains Bill Gates. Gates's Microsoft also owns 30 per cent of Telewest, has a substantial stake in NTL (another cable company), has an interest in Deutsche Telecom and has held talks with Cable & Wireless (C&W), which completes the set of Britain's three major cable companies. However, with C&W's sale of its domestic component to NTL it may not be necessary for Microsoft to take a piece of C&W.

These alliances are based on a commitment to cable that may prove an error. A rival alliance, committed to utilizing super-fast telephone lines, is being constructed by Steve Case of AOL. He is allied with Bell Atlantic and SBC, both local telephone companies; Direct TV, a satellite firm; Philips, who sell set-top boxes; and an off-shoot of Oracle, a software competitor of Microsoft; as well as with Microsoft's other permanent rival, Sun Microsystems. In addition to these allies AOL also now wholly owns Netscape Communications, Microsoft's browser rival, and has acquired Time/Warner. However, alliances are not forever and if either the cable or the telephone strategy proves flawed then expect another rearrangement of alliances. The concern in the telecom industry is that the alliances and partnerships are de facto cartels. Greater consumer awareness is pressurizing governments into legislating – and more importantly, enforcing the legislation – much more rigorously to ensure that price-fixing and abuse of market dominance are constrained.

What is true of alliances is also true of acquisitions. They must be pursued only if they add value to the strategic imperative. Synergy is an overused word but in this instance it perfectly describes the perceived outcome that should drive acquisitions. It is not enough to expand simply for its own sake. This can lead to dis-aggregation, re-aggregation, rationalization, consolidation and the plethora of other tactics for expanding and contracting organizations. For example, the market looked favourably on Ford's acquisition of Kwik-Fit because it was seen as diversifying from a core business with extremely narrow margins. Similarly NTL's bid for Workplace Technologies (WPT) was

> **in all alliances, partnerships, mergers and acquisitions the question must always be, 'does the proposed relationship add synergy?'**

seen as an excellent fit. WPT designs and builds corporate networks, so NTL will be able to offer its customers a single-stop communications service and WPT will be able to boost the technology investments necessary to broaden its capabilities. In contrast to the fit-driven approach, Vivendi has resorted to the grab-all approach. During 1999 it bought utilities companies, as well as taking stakes in entertainment and broadcasting businesses. It is difficult to see where the purchase of an American water utility company fits into the Vivendi plan, especially when Vivendi is simultaneously selling off $20 billion worth of businesses. Its policy smacks of restructuring and expanding at the same time. While its policy in the telecoms sphere looks sound, it may founder on the over-ambitious sorties into other markets. The same was true of BAe's unseemly purchase and subsequent sale of Rover in a short five-year period. In all alliances, partnerships, mergers and acquisitions the question must always be, 'Does the proposed relationship add synergy?' If the answer is not an unequivocal yes, then reject it.

stakeholders

Stakeholders are not an easy group to define because they exist as a consequence of their own perceptions. Whether they call themselves fans, interest groups, pressure groups or stakeholders it is they who perceive themselves as being entitled to a say in how the organization operates. Stakeholder value (STV) is seen as the antithesis of shareholder value. Advocates for STV argue that wealth is created by people working together and recognizing basic human priorities. In other words it is an inclusive enterprise in which ownerships confers not only rights but obligations to the community. In this sense the entire community become stakeholders in all organizations. Businesses are, therefore, forced to accept that they are social institutions and not merely chips in the stock-market game. They need to recognize that the majority of organizations exist somewhere between the state and the individual. The choice is never simply between the two extremes: there is an interconnectedness that binds businesses, suppliers, customers, hospitals, quangos, charities and others in such a way that, to varying degrees, all are stakeholders of each other. Naturally the stake each individual or group has in each organization will differ. Businesses that attempt to operate in a social vacuum will eventually suffer.

complementors

The final group that supports the organization is what Nalebuff and Brandenburger (1996) call the complementors – a 'player is your complementor if customers value your product *more* when they have the other player's product than when they have your product alone'. So, for the take-away fish-and-chip shop, Sarsons and Saxa would be complementors. Similarly, with the advent of Internet shopping, retail outlets have to provide customers with complementary reasons for shopping there. For example, people are actually spending more time in bookshops now than before the existence of Amazon.com. Why? Because bookshops recognized the threat and provided space for in-house coffee shops. Thus Waterstones and Coffee Republic are complementors. It is also true that Amazon.com and Waterstones are complementors since Amazon advertised books per se, not simply their own. To qualify as a complementor, the relationship must be reciprocal: a supermarket without a car park is as ineffective as a car park in the middle of nowhere.

influencers

Complementors act reciprocally with organizations; influencers do not. The most important members of this group are the regulators – those who interpret and enforce the rules of the game. The difference between influencers and supporters is the relative lack of reciprocity: influencers can affect an organization without necessarily being affected themselves. As well as the regulators, this category includes adjudicators and arbitrators, for example ACAS and indeed the law courts themselves. It also includes the professional organizations such as the Confederation of British Industry (CBI), the British Chambers of Commerce (BCC), the Institute of Directors (IoD) and the Federation of Small Businesses, which lobby the authorities on behalf of their members.

competitors

The final set of players is an organization's competitors. There are a variety of ways to define the term 'competitor'. The conventional economics-driven view is that organizations are competitors when customers treat their products or services as close substitutes. Using this view, it is the customer who defines the competitors. However, if the organizations themselves fail to recognize this definition it becomes meaningless. It is more accurate to define competitors as those significant players who perceive themselves, or others, to be competitors, or when they act in ways that would lead others to so define them. This definition must also include the criteria that lead to perceptions of competitor status. It may well be that the main criterion *is* perception; so the competitive status of, say, Microsoft and AOL is merely a reflection of a clash of egos involving Steve Case and Bill Gates. Nalebuff and Brandenburger's definition goes further: they define competitors as those players who cause 'customers to value your product *less* when they have other players' products than when they have your product alone'.

Organizations therefore need to identify their own product more precisely and then question how else customers might satisfy demands for that product. Thus, competitors for business-class seats on British Airways may not only be other airline providers but possibly also 'virtual' meeting facilities such as video-conferencing and the Internet. Similarly, the levelling of spirits sales in the American drinks market over the last 15 years might be a consequence of a growth in the narcotics market. This is because alcohol and drugs provide essentially the same product. This is why identification of the precise product is so important. Are Coca-Cola or Pepsi's products just thirst-quenchers? Clearly not, because if they were their unassailable rival would be free tap water. Even more obviously tap water is also *not* a competitor to Perrier or Evian. Why not? Because Coke, Perrier, Pepsi and Evian are selling something more than a hydration product. They are selling life-style, image and dreams. That is why all four are genuine competitors.

Organizations have to identify precisely who their competitors are in order to be able to resist them. With our definition of competition the organization can rate and measure players more accurately. Where, for example, peer group assessments tend to measure like with like in categories such as fast-moving consumer goods or consumer-packaged goods, our system compares customer needs as its benchmark. The same process can also be used when identifying supply-side competition. There you ask whether you are less attractive to a supplier if it supplies only you, than when it supplies

organizations have to identify precisely who their competitors are in order to be able to resist them

you and another customer. One of the most obvious examples is the competition for capital, which does not take place within industries but across them.

The more traditional way of viewing competitors can lead to price wars and is useful only to those wishing to monopolize the market. Even then, unfair competitive practices are so heavily regulated in the developed economies that completely ruthless competition is often counter-productive. Competitive advantage derives from early identification of true competitors and rugged but legal competitive strategies aimed at retaining or improving competitive status.

This chapter on significant others has highlighted six categories that the business game player needs to understand and identify. Each category has its own subcategories that are also significant, the study of which is repaid by improved performance in the game. Knowledge of *all* players is essential. Neglect them at your peril.

rules

how are games regulated?

Know the exact boundaries of the rules and play to their limits. If that doesn't bring success, change the rules.

When we asked our interviewees to tell us the most important thing they needed to know to be successful at game playing, a large majority opted for *rules*. They argued that detailed knowledge of the rules is essential – not only if you intend to comply with them, but also if you intend to break them. Bill Stealey, the owner of Interactive Magic, put it very concisely:

All games have rules and the people who win most often are the ones who find a way to either expand the rules, bend the rules, make the rules or convince everybody that the rules are slightly different than what they all read on the back of the box.

John Kay (*Sunday Times*, 4 July 1999) said that 'entrepreneurs need fewer rules, not more words'. He argued that the Blair Government's actions in implementing policies such as the minimum wage and the working time directive were making life much harder for the entrepreneur. Such comments are typical of knee-jerk reactions to virtually any new legislation that alters conditions in favour of the workforce, and particularly any that might have been generated by the European Union. Even Michael Portillo has now reversed the Tory stance on the minimum wage. They are also indicative of a failure to analyze adequately the myriad alternative scenarios that any rule changes may trigger.

This leads to having constantly to change policy in order to react to the altered state of the environment, rather than pre-planning at leisure. In the early 1980s, for example, the Conservatives were determined to avoid a repetition of the 1973 crash which they attributed, in part, to restrictive exchange controls. They therefore removed those controls. This unshackling of capital allowed the bankers effectively to reconstruct the golden age of capitalism when unions were unable and governments were unwilling to restrain entrepreneurs. The bankers became so powerful that they were able to influence the government disproportionately. However, on 19 October 1987, Black Monday, the stock market crashed with a fall of 20 per cent recorded overnight. Stocks had been hugely overvalued and the cycle started seven years earlier by the Conservatives had been completed. A failure to anticipate the effects of rule changes had led to roller-coaster consequences for the economy. With it came a recognition of the vulnerability of governments to global economic forces, as well as an understanding that locally directed rule changes can actually reverberate around the system and devastate the originator's own economy. What the exchange control case demonstrated was the potential power of rules, even in relatively fluid games such as business.

However, did John Kay have a point? Surely, rules *do* constrain? Wrong! Only bad rules constrain: good rules *en*able and no rules *dis*able. Rules are created by the players for the sole purpose of enabling the game to be played. The only thing they constrain is chaos. Rules are the mechanism we use to ensure that the game continues to be played and is worth playing.

Some business writers argue that what distinguishes business from other games is the dynamic nature of the rules in business. Nalebuff and Brandenburger (1996), for example, state that business is different from other games in a fundamental way because it 'doesn't stand still … While football, poker and chess have ultimate ruling bodies … business doesn't'. Although Nalebuff and Brandenburger concede that governments do impose anti-trust laws and other regulations, they say this represents 'only a small portion of the rules by which business is played' and that people 'are free to change the game of business to their benefit'. We agree that business rules are dynamic, but so are the rules of every game. If the rules preclude enjoyable and successful game playing they will be changed. More significant, however, is our disagreement that the regulations established by governing bodies account for only a small portion of the rules by which business is played. Theoretically Nalebluff and Brandenburger may be right, but the impact of the regulations established by the Department of Trade and Industry (DTI), the Office of Fair Trading (OFT) and the Competition Commission (CC, formerly the Monopolies and Mergers Commission) is now of paramount importance. Just ask Bill Gates or Rupert Murdoch how important governmental agencies can be in the game.

If we accept that rules are inevitable then what the game player needs to understand is what types of rules there are. Also, how are these rules created and by whom, and how are they enforced, and how can they be manipulated to best advantage?

natural rules

Essentially there are only three types of rule: the *natural*, the *stated* and the *unstated*. By natural rules we mean the laws of nature. Although these laws are apparently immutable, they can nevertheless be subject to change in the light of greater knowledge. In recent years, for example, the generally accepted concept of Gaussian distribution (the bell-shaped curve), which is used by probability analysts to predict the probability of rare events, has come under challenge. Insurers use the technique to calculate premiums that protect against catastrophes; therefore, any challenge to what has been seen as a 'natural' rule could have far-reaching effects. Researchers have now found what they consider might be a new universal law, linking phenomena as diverse as floods, ecosystems and mineral deposits. Evidence in all these fields suggest a distribution curve much flatter that the bell-shaped curve. This means that rare events are more common than the bell shape suggests. In Fig. 4.1, which relates to rare species in forests, it is obvious that the left side of the new curve predicts that it is more likely that rare species will be found than the occurrence predicted by the bell-shaped curve. According to Professor Turcotte of Cornell University (turcotte@geology.cornell.edu) the new curve explains the apparently higher-than-expected occurrences of hurricanes, floods and fires in the last decade. Insurance companies may, therefore, have been using an inaccurate natural law as a predictor and so their 'rare' events appear rarer than is the case. Insurers will no doubt increase premiums on the off-chance that the research is right. This illustrates the real problem with natural rules: ultimately they cannot be disobeyed. If it turns out they can, then the rule was wrong and a new rule will need to be established.

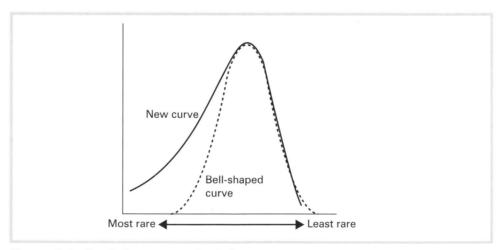

Figure 4.1   Predicting rare species in forests

Source: Professor John Harte, University of California at Berkeley (jharte@socrates.Berkeley.edu)

Rules only have to be changed quickly and reactively if there is insufficient flexibility in the current rules. This brings us to another 'natural' law: Ashby's 'Law of Requisite Variety'. In his work on cybernetics (1956) Ashby argues that only by balancing the amount of variety (complexity) in the system to be controlled with the variety in the regulator that seeks to control that system, can the control be exercised harmoniously. The solution is to provide balance by either increasing variety in the regulator (amplification) or decreasing it in the system (attenuation). As Ashby says, 'only variety destroys variety'.

Why should businesses care about such esoteric ideas? Because they go to the heart of organizational knowledge, especially the planning aspects. Similarly, anyone with responsibility for the survival of their organization would be well advised to consult the early work done on cybernetics and systems because it deals with natural laws of organizational behaviour. As the inventor of the term 'cybernetics' explained, it is the 'science of communication and control in the animal and machine' (Weiner, 1948). Whilst the systems approach has been given some contemporary business credibility by Peter Senge (1994), cybernetics has been corrupted by its sci-fi connotations. In reality Weiner used the term very precisely. Its Greek root suggests 'steersmanship', which entails continuous feedback and adjustment in order to stay on course – precisely the skills required by any CEO, manager, supervisor or operator in the modern business game.

So, natural rules must be in the knowledge bank of the expert player; if they are not, then they must be learned quickly. It is also true that certain rules take on the characteristics of natural rules, but there are exceptions and this is where risk analysts, or professional gamblers as we prefer to call them, come into it. Players must know the risks (the odds) in order to either abide by

you can only be a risk taker if you know the odds

them or reject them. You can only be a risk taker if you know the odds. There is a difference between bravery and ignorance. It is sensible to bet on Goliath and not David, but only if you had no knowledge of the kid's ability with a sling-shot. A gambling friend of ours from New York also used the Bible to explain his attitude to risk. He said: 'The race may not always be to the swift nor the battle to the strong [Ecclesiastes 9:7] but that's where the smart money goes.' In other words, play the percentages. All game players must know the natural rules, including probability, that govern their game.

Stated and unstated rules

A knowledge of the stated and unstated rules is also essential. By stated rules we mean all the explicit laws, codes of practice, treaties and contracts that affect the game in which an organization or an individual is involved. By unstated we mean the implicit conventions and assumptions that are embedded in the fabric of the game. The implicit rules tend to be those that deal with the essence of the game, while the explicit deal with its smooth operation.

There is a cycle in which stated and unstated rules are established and supplant each other as the needs of the game demand. Imagine, for example, that in a busy restaurant there are 'in' and 'out' doors by which the waiters enter and leave the kitchen. Often these doors are unmarked but everyone knows the rules, and they benefit everyone for obvious reasons. One day a new waiter is employed who insists on going through the wrong doors. Despite verbal admonitions he continues with this anti-social practice claiming, quite rightly, that there is no rule in his contract or in work practice that precludes his behaviour. Solution? Sack him. But actually he is a good waiter and you want to keep him. An alternative solution would be to renegotiate his contract and write into it a 'door rule'. The hope would be that eventually the rule would once more become so accepted and commonplace that the need to have a stated rule would diminish to the point of extinction. It would sink back into the deep-seated and unstated rules that govern all cultures. There exists, therefore, a cycle of unstated and stated rules that are intrinsically connected. As Fig. 4.2 shows, there are stages in the development of rules, in which players at first comply, then test and then transgress the implicit rules. The transgression transforms into the first stage of the explicit rules, then that stage merges into testing and then compliance. In this model, the dominance of unstated rules denotes a relatively homogenous society, whereas the dominance of stated rules denotes a society probably in transition.

We believe this to be analogous to the problems with corporate culture. Organizations try to move from one corporate culture to another without the behavioural modifications that can only be generated by stated rules. They also fail to understand the need to pass through the modification period, in other words to change the climate. Take the concept of positive discrimination, for example. If we look at gender or race, we at first recognize a problem – racism or sexism. We respond by putting in place stated rules (for example, quotas, affirmative action, positive discrimination) that change the climate, but they do not change the culture – racists and sexists still exist. Gradually, we hope, the enforcement of stated rules leads to general compliance and an eventual realization that racism and sexism are wrong. If that happens then stated rules become unstated and the culture has been changed. The problem is that the climatic period tends to be long and tortuous and those being discriminated against are naturally impatient. Splits appear within their ranks between moderates and radicals, between Martin Luther King and Malcolm X for instance. The problem can be redefined during these internal battles and new allegiances formed to pursue new strategies. This is why rules tend

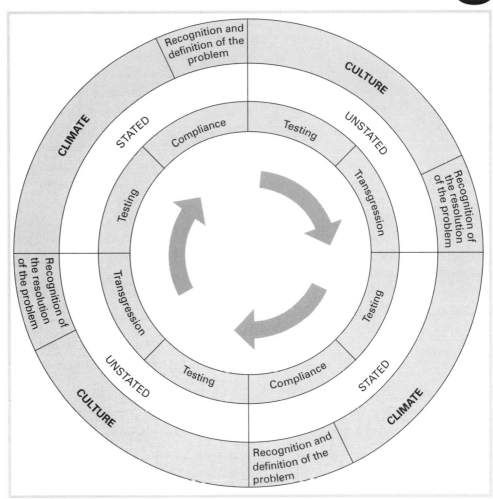

Figure 4.2   Stages in the development of rules

not to apply equally to groups, because the groups are located at different positions on the climate/culture cycle and therefore they define the issues differently.

stated rules

All rules, whether stated or unstated, are aimed at maintaining a level of stability or order so that we can continue playing. Therefore, when players are thinking of creating rules, or changing them, they should ask: do they enhance the game? If the answer is no, or even maybe, then wait or run a pilot scheme. If no pilot arena is available then some sort of simulation model must be created. This is especially true in an era when the power of regulatory bodies (such as OFWAT, OFTEL etc.) is beginning to be exercised more forcefully. Rules are changing virtually overnight, for example in competition law. The most important point to note about the Competition Commission is that it even exists. Why, in a capitalist system, should competition be regulated? Surely capitalism is synonymous with competition? True, but unbridled competition is like unbridled war – it is catastrophic. The Competition Commission (http://www.compe-

all rules are aimed at maintaining a level of stability or order so that we can continue playing

tition-commission.gov.uk) exists to maintain the game. It aims to enforce the new Competition Act (1 March 2000) which itself seeks to strengthen competition laws by prohibiting actions by organizations that prevent, restrict or distort competition. It also prohibits the abuse of dominant positions by organizations. In the major provisions of the Competition Act 1998, published by the Office of Fair Trading (http://www.oft.gov.uk), these prohibitions are, in turn, based on articles 8 and 82 of the ratified Treaty of Amsterdam (http://www.europe.eu.int). This link with European Union (EU) regulations allows the British authorities to deal with transgressions of the Act in a manner that ensures consistency with EU law. As such, the damaging and costly counter-rulings that result from the application of EU law *after* British judgements can be avoided. Thus we find at least one compelling reason for the acquisition of detailed knowledge of stated rules – it saves money.

Imagine, for the moment, Rupert Murdoch contemplating the acquisition of Manchester United and asking himself and his team, 'How much do we know about anti-competitive agreements?' The team might think such agreements would include price-fixing, production control, market sharing, application of dissimilar conditions or subsequently obligated contractual agreements. They would be right. However, there is another more important aspect of the Act. It is the rule of 'appreciable effect' and it has an effect upon all the rules stated above. Who decides whether an appreciable effect has, or is likely to, occur? The Director General of Fair Trading (DGFT). Has he any guidelines? Yes. Generally, an agreement will have no appreciable effect on competition if the partners' combined share of the relevant market does not exceed 25 per cent. But the DGFT takes the view that certain agreements – price-fixing, imposition of minimum resale prices and networked agreements – can 'have an appreciable effect even where the combined market share falls below the 25 per cent threshold'. Even more confusingly, the DGFT may find that the effect on competition (of parties with a combined market share greater than 25 per cent) is *not* appreciable.

Confused? You will be if you do not locate and understand stated rules. It is no good saying that your lawyers will sort it out. They sort out the detail. It is for the CEO or project manager to point the lawyers in the right direction. In the case of the Competition Act what the stated rules actually say, with monotonous regularity, is, 'if the DG *considers*', 'the DG *may* find', 'the DG will *generally* regard', 'if, *in the view* of the DG'. In other words the *opinion* of the DGFT *becomes* stated law. Therefore, you need to gather information about those factors likely to influence the opinion of the DGFT – especially the views of the DGFT's political boss at the DTI. So some knowledge of the stated rules must be a prerequisite to playing the game and business players tend to ignore this basic premise. Nobody would dream of playing chess or tennis without first establishing precisely what the rules are.

unstated rules

While stated rules are the benchmark that ensures the game can be played to a minimum level, it is the unstated rules that guarantee the game can be played to an optimal level. Take the gay issue in the military. A stated rule is that gays are banned. An unstated rule is that we know there are gays in the military, just don't get caught. To be even more precise, if you don't show yourself we will not come looking for you. Perversely, this unstated rule was actually stated in the US military when Clinton issued his 'Don't ask, don't tell' policy.

The influence of such rules is not always malign, but that is not the point. Whether benign, malign or neutral, what is important about such rules is that they are not easily available for inspection. Businesses will often accept, for example, that unstated rules differ from society to society, between the US and the UK, between France and Japan for instance. However, they will miss or ignore the difference between middle management and worker. Why? Because it is more subtle, more subliminal. In Fig. 4.2 we used the term 'culture' as virtually synonymous with unstated rules because that is how cultures are transmitted. When someone new arrives in an organization it is not the stated rules that transmit the organisation's underlying ethics. It is no coincidence, for example, that the phrase 'canteen culture' was so prevalent in the debate surrounding institutional racism in the police. The argument put forward by racial equality campaigns has been that despite the publication of copious 'stated' rules, the canteen culture has not been altered. What the conscientious corporate players need to understand is what makes up the underlying culture.

Defining culture is notoriously difficult, but generally definitions include such elements as a common language, common history, common appearance and ethics. A deep understanding of these elements is essential to the player hoping to succeed in any game. It is in these elements that the unstated rules live. Diverse language rules are, for example, very obvious between 'alien' cultures. Haru Yamada, a Japanese born academic who has lived extensively in the US, wrote a fascinating book entitled *Different Games, Different Rules* (1997) which dealt with the concept of language as the most powerful cultural transmitter. Interestingly,

Yamada, confirms the significance of language for the business game in the sub-title to her book: *Why Americans and Japanese misunderstand each other.* They misunderstand each other because they apply the rules of their own organization to the language of the other. The other cultural elements – appearance, history, myths and ethics – interact, as equal partners with language, to create the labyrinth of unstated rules that game players must understand.

What the expert player has to do is recognize the unstated rules in the various categories. With appearance, for example, the key work must be appropriateness. Is the way I look appropriate? If you are wearing a clown's outfit and everyone else is naked there are only two alternatives. You are the clown at a nudist camp – in which case you got it right; any other scenario and the chances are you got it wrong. We should re-emphasize here that if you wish to be *in*appropriate you must still know the rules. The same is true of history, mythology (the stories organizations tell about themselves) and, indeed, ethics.

Business organizations are under increasing and sustained pressure to demonstrate ethical behaviour in their conduct. Companies can be penalized directly, by fines, sanctions and closures, or indirectly by investment going elsewhere. In excess of £2 billion is now invested in UK ethical funds. In 1999, for example, there were criminal fines imposed on Roche of Switzerland for its role in a vitamins cartel, and on Whirlpool, the white products company, for misleading investors. There were also punitive damages against General Motors, whilst the pressure brought to bear on Shell over its operations in Nigeria and the North Sea forced the company to alter its operational standards. Issues such as age, gender, disability, sexuality, human rights and race are, to varying degrees, being forced on to the corporate agenda, like it or not.

Race is a particularly emotive issue. In March 1998 a lawsuit was filed against the Boeing Corporation alleging racial discrimination. Boeing, recognizing how difficult it is to make a racial discrimination case stick, refused to release documentation and tried to pay off the plaintiffs. It did not work. One of the plaintiffs managed get hold of a Ku Klux Klan card, which was part of a consignment being distributed in Boeing's Seattle plant, and

ethical considerations are practical considerations for astute business players

he took it to the government. If Boeing are proved to have flouted federal guidelines on racial discrimination it could cost them $11 billion worth of government contracts. Ethical considerations are practical considerations for astute business players.

Ethical issues underline the simultaneous existence of contradictory stated and unstated rules. In 1997, for example, Sears Roebuck were fined $60 million for bankruptcy fraud. Here was an obvious case for the introduction of a stated ethics code administered by a member of one of the 1990s growth professions – ethics officers. The problem was that an ethics officer, an ethics code and an ethics hotline had been in place at Sears Roebuck for three years. The illegal practice of improper debt collection was, according to a Sears spokeswoman, so institutionalized that 'nobody ever called the hotline about it'. In other words, the unstated rules were so powerful that they made the stated rules effectively irrelevant. The job of management is not to produce stated rules in isolation, but to insinuate and effect the unstated rules such that they are synchronized.

Barbara Ley Toffler, head of Arthur Andersen's business ethics group in New York, contends that the reasons most codes are ineffectual is that they do not address the core ethical issue – values. Ethical codes *are* being set up and 100 per cent of Fortune 500 companies and 60 per cent of British companies now have ethics officers, if only to pay lip-service to governmental and pressure group imperatives. But they are not aimed at changing organizational values. Barbara Ley Toffler argues that such compliance modules can actually be counter-productive. Having an ethics and compliance programme that employees perceive exists only to protect the company may be more harmful than having no programme at all. Toffler's comments are echoed by the UK Institute of Directors which has established the Hub Initiative, charged with improving the reputation of business in community. The Hub's CEO said, 'If you want everyone in a business to operate to higher standards, you have to work out what your common purposes and values are and train people in that.' The difficulty then arises as to who regulates these new ethical imperatives. If a company decides to embark on a policy including corporate ethics, it is rarely for altruistic reasons; it wants the world to know it is ethical because it improves image. The more enlightened may actually recognize the performance value of intangible assets, but mostly that is an unexpected bonus. If you want the world to believe you are serious it needs to believe you are adequately monitored. Who polices the policeman, who judges the board?

At the turn of the century, companies began to turn to the 'Big Five' consultancies to perform this auditing task. However, these external auditors still report to the board and not to the shareholders, let alone the stakeholders. Since the board is most likely to be where the problem lies, there is an obvious clash of interest for the consultant. The fact that genuine non-executive directors (NED) are not reporting to shareholders is evidenced by the recommendation of the Turnbull Committee that shareholders' interests should be represented directly to the board in the person of an active, professional and committed NED. The Big Five in their turn are trying to bolster their own ethical credibility by broadening the expertise of their staff base by recruiting staff with skills in the 'softer' management areas. PricewaterhouseCoopers, for example, has a 'business ethicist' on its board and KPMG has a deal with Anita Roddick (of Body Shop) in which KPMG outsources its ethical audit to Body Shop and Body Shop outsources its business audits to KPMG. So everybody is trying with ethics, but it remains a slippery customer. Business can no longer try to isolate itself from societal concerns over ethical issues. Companies ignore the outcry over fat-cat salaries, genetically modified foods and profiteering by privatized utilities at their long-term peril. They must learn to read the unstated rules and understand them as thoroughly as the natural and stated rules. They must then take responsibility for altering those unstated rules by a process that uses a combination of stated rules and unstated example.

In particular, unless rewards and promotions are seen to link with core organizational values, nothing will change. Chris Marsden, of the corporate citizens unit of Warwick Business School, asks the pertinent question: 'Have the performance contracts of the middle management of your organization been rewritten to take into account the goals stated in the code of conduct?' If the answer is no then don't hold your breath for an ethical change in the organization's behaviour. This is precisely what some companies like Microsoft and Levi-Strauss have done by linking ethics to performance. In both companies they have linked bonus schemes to compliance with the core corporate values. It is not considered sufficient to achieve business objectives at the expense of corporate values.

However, not everyone agrees that this approach helps to develop and maintain values. Harry Cohen, the CEO of the consultancy firm SGI, actually scrapped a scheme that rewarded employees for demonstrating certain values. He claimed that the company ended up with some 'top-flight people who became complacent and thought they could back off from delivery and focus on values instead' (*Financial Times*, 7 September 1999). What Cohen is highlighting is the need for appropriate rewards. Employees have to believe that the whole organization is adhering to the value model, including top management. The rewards received need to be personally targeted. However, while it is important to link value to rewards it is even more important to remember that values can only be demonstrated in a company that remains in existence. As Mark Elliott of Levi-Strauss puts it, 'For any company in the business of making money, meeting performance targets remains the most important value of all.'

rule enforcement

If stated and unstated rules are so important, how are they enforced? Unstated rules can only be enforced by the entire group, because transgressions are transgressions against the entire group. Inappropriate actions will be frowned upon and the transgressors will be admonished or ostracized. Individuals will find that group members will begin to ignore them, fail to inform them, fail to support them, promotion will dry up, perks will be withdrawn and they will cease to be genuine members of the group. In the most serious cases the isolation will be achieved by overt and even aggressive actions. This is as true of companies as it is of individuals. Organizations that act against the ethos of associations to which they belong will eventually either come back into line or be disciplined. No one company will be allowed to rock the boat (unless, of course, they are dominant in the market). The associations will turn to the regulators of stated rules for assistance.

Stated rules are different. While they may be the product of the group, the responsibility for enforcement is usually passed to a third party for convenience. This is a recognition that the game would be more effectively played if impartial arbitrators were involved. An interesting exception is when the game is controlled by self-imposed rules. When we asked the self-confessed spin doctor Charlie Whelan whether there were any rules to the spinning game he said, 'Only those I impose upon myself.' When asked what they were, he replied, 'I never lie'. The rule was not 'always tell the truth', but 'never to lie' – say nothing rather than lie. In this type of game the players themselves take on the role of the referee. Where referees, umpires, judges, tribunals and regulators are needed it is to maintain the game. We will collectively refer to this group as *regulators*. These regulators can only enforce the rules by consensus and if the players choose to ignore them their effectiveness is negated. Where this happens the game's administrators will resort to coercion, including the imposition of sanctions up to, and including, dismissal from the game. The ultimate sanctions of disbarring a lawyer or striking off a doctor are examples of the power of the regulators.

> regulators can only enforce the rules by consensus and if the players choose to ignore them their effectiveness is negated

To illustrate the importance of regulators, look at the way in which companies attempt to manipulate the stated rules. In France, the regulator responsible for financial stability is the CECEI. In August 1999 the CECEI, at 4.15 am after an 11-hour meeting, made the following statement concerning the attempted take-over of Société Generale (SG) by Banque Nationale de Paris (BNP): 'In view of the results of the [take-over] offer, BNP does not have effective control of SG. In spite of efforts [by the two banks] it was not possible to reach a clear and concerted industrial solution.' The basis of the CECEI's decision was that BNP had only secured 31.8 per cent of SG's voting rights. In the opinion of the regulator this did not constitute control. Had the buy-out team of BNP misjudged the likely decision of the CECEI? The answer is probably that it did. It may have miscalculated the political effect on the CECEI of the presence on the streets of hundreds of SG workers demonstrating against the take-over. It may have miscalculated the effect on the CECEI of pressure from the bankers who viewed the judgement as a victory for shareholder value. What is clear is the powerful role the regulator plays in the outcome of the game. In Tony Blair's first two years in power his government created 12 new inspectorates. These were in addition to the rationalization of private-sector regulation like the Financial Services Authority (FSA), which now encompasses nine former regulators.

If the state insists on certain standards in the private and public sector but relinquishes operational control of the processes, then the only way to attempt to retain control is by regulating the output. Either way the manpower resources will be the same. Margaret Thatcher tried to circumvent a natural law (Ashby, 1956). She thought that it was possible to attenuate complexity in one part of the system (government) without compensating for that dilution elsewhere in the system. You may be able to redistribute the regulatory load but you cannot radically reduce it. What creates or destroys workload is the efficacy of the rules. There are simple but often ignored guidelines when deciding whether or not to create a rule:

- Is it necessary? In other words do people actually walk on the grass? If they do not, then why prohibit it?

- If it is necessary, what are the costs of enforcing it? If they are too great then don't have the rule and think of another solution. Concrete over the grass, for example.

- Never make threats you cannot back up. There is nothing so damaging as inconsistency – you can never recover.

The simplest advice for those who have to play by the rules is to use as their guidelines the reverse logic of the guidelines for the rule-makers:

- If there is not a rule, do not force the rule-makers to create one by your behaviour. Don't walk on the grass unless absolutely necessary.

- Estimate the rule-makers' costs of enforcing the rule and make a subsequent cost–benefit analysis. For example, it may cost less to accumulate parking fines than bother to find parking spaces and paying; it may cost less to take an occasional £10 fine rather than pay rail fares.

- Try to anticipate the regulator's alternatives and plan for them. If you calculate the rule is too costly to enforce, so eventually, might the regulator.

An important issue for the game player must, therefore, be the regulators themselves and their personalities and agendas. They are becoming a tougher and more aggressive breed. When Tom Winsor was appointed as Britain's rail regulator in 1999, he said that his first priority was to meet a complacent railway head-on.

Joel Klein, the top enforcer of anti-trust laws in the US, has been called by *Wall Street Journal* as 'the most active and most feared Washington regulator in a generation'. He has filed more anti-trust suits in his short tenure than any of his predecessors over the previous 20 years. Cases include that of Microsoft case and the predatory pricing case against American Airlines (AA). The reason Klein is the most feared is his willingness to rewrite the rules in order to take on the business giants. The AA case in particular is seen by many analysts as unwinnable, but Klein is ploughing on. The merger frenzy of the late 1990s forced regulators like Klein to the view that only radical new competition rules could counter-balance the rapidly changing business world. It is vital that business players have detailed knowledge of industry regulators.

One of our interviewees, ICI's chief executive, Brendan O'Neill, pointed out that while role playing of competitors, partners and collaborators is taken very seriously when companies make key strategic decisions, the relevant regulator rarely gets sufficient attention. As O'Neill jokingly asked, 'Who wants to play the referee?' Sir Peter Middeton of Barclays qualified O'Neill's comments by saying that what generally happened was that a company's first contact with the regulator was usually disastrous but they got better at it very quickly. 'Look at the utilities,' he said. 'They have become masters at dealing with regulators.' The business player must be able to identify the influences that are likely to reflect the regulators' decisions. Players must understand that the regulators are political animals. Whilst Tom Winsor denies he might be subject to political pressures, he also admits that 'passengers are voters'. A well-known Labour supporter, Winsor was selected by Tony Blair personally. Winsor himself describes his role as a 'referee'. 'The Strategic Rail Authority … will be a player in the industry,' he said, but 'I am the referee.' Even if Winsor does not understand that the referee *is* a player, business people need to do so or risk disastrous consequences.

This chapter has demonstrated the complexity of the interaction between the natural, stated and unstated rules. Corporate players must understand where, on the rules cycle, they and the other players are located. Then they can focus most usefully on the type of rule changes that need to be made. Wherever that focus is directed, players also need to identify and understand who makes the rules and who enforces them. Having such knowledge will not guarantee success in the game – but not having it will guarantee failure.

chapter 5

environment

where are we playing?

Assess the environment in which your game will be played and then prepare that environment for your advantage.

When you imagine any sporting event one of the first things you think of is the playing arena. The wide open spaces of a cricket field; the frightening approach to the 18th hole at Carnoustie; the tight confines of a squash court; the intense intimacy of a chess board; the loneliness of a diving board. Add to these the natural elements of rain, wind, sun, humidity, altitude, temperature and texture of playing surface and you have the variables that make up the *environment* of the game being played. The environment consists of those factors over which players have only marginal control; in most instances it consists of factors to which players must adapt.

As with *rules*, if an environmental factor threatens to ruin the game then players will attempt to eliminate it or postpone the game. Messing with the environment can, however, be messing with the game. Take artificial surfaces, for example. In tennis and field hockey they have been a massive success. In football, however, they never caught on. In football they damaged the essence of the game, whereas in hockey the change of surface enhanced the essence of the game. Interestingly, the change in the game of hockey became so significant that the rules had to be changed to accommodate the differences. So players can not only use the environment to their advantage, but actually change it.

Cricket pitches are regularly doctored to favour playing strengths and in the NFL crowds are encouraged to make a noise so that opposing quarterbacks can not call the plays. In military combat, the heavy bombardment of enemy positions very precisely prepares the environment to be more suitable for your troops. General Sir Michael Rose, the

Commanding Officer of the 22nd Special Air Service Regiment (SAS) during the Iranian Embassy siege, spoke to us at length about the crucial importance of preparation of the environment in any military operation before commanders are able to proceed with a mission. On occasions they naturally have to enter an unprepared environment if circumstances so dictate, in which case soldiers will rely on previously rehearsed drills. Business players must do precisely the same – prepare the environment if possible, fall back on rehearsed routines if it is not.

The environment can alter as a result of technological intervention or geographical considerations. One of the factors that made the Gulf War relatively straightforward in comparison with Kosovo, for example, was the terrain. The mountainous, wooded and sodden environment of Kosovo required a level of ground-force commitment far greater and, more importantly, far earlier than the flat, open, desert of the Gulf War. A considerable amount of work would have been needed in order to make the Kosovan environment more friendly. As both Napoleon and Hitler found to their cost, you may be able to defeat the Russian army but you cannot defeat the Russian winter.

Another crucial environmental issue is time. How much time that is left to complete the game fundamentally alters players' perceptions of the situation. Consistently overestimating the speed with which projects can be completed costs millions of pounds in penalty clauses pay-backs to dissatisfied customers. It is a problem dealt with superbly in Eliyahu Goldratt's managerial novel *The Goal* (1992). Unrealistic time estimates are expensive to everybody concerned with an enterprise – 'time kills deals'. It is also important not to overestimate how long it will take to close a deal or, indeed, to allow time to pass without appropriate action occurring. It can also be effective, on occasion, actually to delay matters until the environment is right for you. Prolonging negotiations can allow the heat to go out of a situation.

Time is an environmental issue because it can both generate and alter mood. Mood has an unpredictable and yet powerful influence on the game. For example, the statement, 'the stock market lost confidence today', is a comment about a mood swing. Identifying or even predicting what will affect mood must, therefore, give players an advantage.

In games, then, there are three environmental factors to consider. The first is *atmospheric* – is it raining, sunny, windy? What are the climatic conditions in which the game is played? Where are we playing – are we somewhere we know or a place with which we are unfamiliar? The second is *mood* – what is the prevailing mood of the significant players? How much time have they got left to complete the game? Finally, there is *technology* – has the equipment been changed or improved? Have the facilities or playing surface been altered? These are the issues with which business players must also contend. Their problem is that the pace of business change is frenetic

– partly because the rewards are so high, but mostly because the game is relatively unstructured. There is no procedure for change and so it can, as a consequence, take on a momentum of its own before its value to the game can be adequately assessed. Nevertheless, by treating the environment analytically its worst excesses can be either neutralized or utilized by the clever player.

atmosphere

In business it rarely matters, as it does in sport on a daily basis, whether it is raining or its dry. However, this does not mean that atmospheric factors are irrelevant. One of the least researched aspects of working in a foreign country, for example, is the weather. Is it hot? If so, how does local business cope with the heat? Do they close down at 2 pm, do they start work at 7 am? Will you continue to work to your timetable or will you adapt? Is there a rainy season during which transportation difficulties might affect delivery schedules? Can you sell the populace sun-screen or skis or waterproof clothing? How do you market your product? In Nigeria, for instance, Guinness is sold chilled and marketed as a refresher, in much the same way as lager is in the UK. Incidentally, imported Nigerian Guiness is sold to Nigerian immigrants in South London.

However, the rapidity with which the weather changes does provide a useful analogy. While hurricanes, droughts, floods and other climatic events are, by their nature, random, they are, nevertheless predictable in a macro sense. Why cannot the same care be taken in dealing with random social events such as occur in the political or business domain? Is it not the case that certain political regions could be considered as inherently unstable – the Balkans, for example? The evidence is strong. Would it not be sensible in such regions to put in place some sort of political hurricane watch? If so, why is it not done?

Similarly, in business an early analysis of the volatility of particular markets is a major environmental issue. Depressions, recessions and crashes are random events in the business game, but they will occur, so in that sense they are predictable. The organization that includes such events into their planning cycles is the one that will be the least surprised and best able to deal with them. For example, one of the 'surprises' that is mentioned by virtually every interviewee in our BMW/Rover case study is the 'high pound'. While the pound was unusually high it was not 'uniquely' high. It was within a predictable range. Were the calculations by BMW strategists sufficiently risk-averse or did they take a gamble on the pound staying within a certain range? If so it was a reasonable gamble but it has to be recognized as precisely that – a gamble. What needs to be understood in such cases is that the crucial decision is not whether or not to buy Rover but whether or not to gamble.

Many Lloyds 'names', for example, had lost sight of this simple fact and were consequently extremely surprised to lose money, to the extent that they lobbied the government to come to their assistance. The Lloyds 'names' might be forgiven for losing sight of the impredictability of their game since for years they had come to view their 'winnings' as 'earnings'. Incidentally, not many of the 'working names' lost money. They were close enough to the game to remain aware of its underlying volatility and off-load their risk on to other, more naïve, players.

These are all examples of macro-environmental factors. On a more localized level players need to be aware of the effect of working conditions. Will operators do better or worse in certain conditions? Will they strike if the temperature is too hot or too cold? Can they be made more productive and simultaneously more satisfied? Does the layout of the workplace liberate or constrain? If it is open plan, is that for everybody or do the senior management have their own offices? If you hot-desk or even hot-office, as do some of the major consultancies, does it work? If productivity is up, has retention also improved, or is the reverse true? In other words are there positive, negative or neutral correlations? Does the workplace environment enhance or diminish performance? The most important step in the process of adding competitive advantage is to ask the right questions in the pre-decision phase. Generally the answers tend to be common sense, although sometimes they can be revolutionary. Both types add to organizational effectiveness. Brendan O'Neill (ICI) admits to being desperate to relocate the corporate HQ because he recognizes how the current premises are incompatible with the corporate environment he wishes to create as part of a rejuvenated corporate culture. The huge atrium at the Millbank offices is not conducive to the socialization that is so important in the development and maintenance of corporate identity.

> the most important step in the process of adding competitive advantage is to ask the right questions in the pre-decision phase

Spatial configurations tend to reinforce hierarchical structures and they also affect electronic traffic. Senior staff tend to attract, but not respond to e-mails, whereas the favourite medium of juniors is electronic. Such non-face-to-face communication confirms hierarchies and can isolate senior management intellectually, emotionally and strategically from their staff. Atmospheric factors, as we have defined them, are relatively undermentioned in managerial literature – with the exception of the feng-shui brigade. But business players neglect atmosphere at considerable, if often intangible, cost.

mood

Mood is the mental attitude that prevails in the game. On a simple level, mood can be the result of the prevailing atmosphere. Ambience is an important mood determinant, hence the term 'mood-setter'. Every business player knows the importance of putting customers, clients, even competitors, at their ease. Equally, it can be just as important to make your opponent ill at ease and uncomfortable. When it became apparent to bookshops that Internet sellers could provide greater choice and convenience for the customer, then the big players like Waterstones and Barnes and Noble reinvented the ambience of their shops to be more comfortable and welcoming. The introduction of coffee shops, reading tables and a generally more convivial mood enabled the booksellers to provide the one product with which their Internet competitors could not compete – mood.

Another determinant of mood is the time available to complete a task. Remember the frenetic response of Alex Ferguson as time began to ebb away in the European Cup Final. There was also a hiatus when he effectively conceded defeat and the mood changed to resignation. This was, of course, followed by elation when the winning goals went in during injury time. The mood changes on the Manchester United and Bayern Munich benches over that 110 minutes of so, illustrated, in a highly condensed form, the way in which time can affect mood.

Perhaps more significantly for business is the time frame in which business is expected to be conducted. While most organizations claim to have strategic visions that stretch into the future, the reality is that business games rarely last more than two or three years – the time it takes an individual to move on. Where is the incentive for any executives to take a long-term approach to an organization that will actually judge them in the short term? The emphasis on shareholder value

it is up to the senior management to identify accurately the real game for the long-term health of the organization

can both create and reinforce short-termism. It need not do so, of course, if the shareholders are prepared to forego dividends, but that is not a common occurrence. As a consequence, the deals that produce immediate increases in shareholder value are the deals that will be encouraged. It is, therefore, in the interest of the player to hide any negative long-term effects of positive short-term policies. The perceived time-frame of the game is distorting the actions of the players. The message they are receiving is that short-termism will be rewarded. The problem is often that the game has been incorrectly defined. Winning the next match might stave off the sack today for the incumbent manager but it may not help with the long-term health of the organization. It is up to the senior management, at the policy level, to identify accurately the real game for the long-term health of the organization. This is just as difficult for them since they will probably move on in the short-term, particularly if they are in publicly quoted companies. However, this is not the case where individuals or families retain effective control of the organization. As our case study on a BMW shows, the emotional long-term attachment to the company by the controlling family can be the most important factor in any analysis of the company itself.

In his latest book, Bill Gates (1999) points to speed of communication as being the most important factor of the next decade. Gates argues that while the 1980s were about quality and the 1990s about re-engineering, the 2000s will be about 'velocity': not only about how quickly business itself will be conducted but also about how quickly the process of business will transform. Ironically, Gates invokes the metaphor of the human nervous system as the model for the future company. One of the early gurus of cybernetic management, Stafford Beer (1995), created his 'viable systems model' on precisely the same premise. What Gates has realized is that digital technology has made the visionary ideas of Beer more realizable. As both Gates and Beer have pointed out, the human nervous system is the most effective model known to us for dealing with complexity. For Stafford Beer the function of the nervous system, digital or otherwise, is to ensure the survivability of the system; for Gates it means not only that, but also adds a competitive edge over others who ignore it. As Gates says:

Companies need to have that same kind of nervous system [as human beings]: the ability to run smoothly and efficiently; to respond quickly to emergencies and opportunities; to quickly get valuable information to the people in the company who need it; the ability to make decisions quickly and interact with customers. A biological nervous system triggers your reflexes so that you can react quickly to danger or need. It gives you the information you need as you ponder issues and make choices. You're alert to the most important things, and your nervous system blocks out information that isn't important.

What both Beer and Gates illustrate is that the speed with which information can be processed will radically change the mood of not only the business world but of every other aspect of life. Time, then, is clearly a key environmental factor.

The mood of a game can also be changed by the introduction of a new player. The mood of the airline industry, for example, has been radically altered by new players not technology. Players like Freddie Laker, People Express, Branson and Easy Jet have made the bigger carriers react. They altered the mood in the industry. Compaq, Microsoft and Apple did the same to an industry previously dominated by the juggernaut IBM. Mood, climate and culture represent stages in the evolution of the prevailing ethos of the game. They are equivalent to short,

medium and long-term alterations in that ethos. Mood can change almost instantaneously and, if it does not find support, it can change back.

technology

By altering the physical environment, technological innovations lay the foundations for eventual cultural shifts. If, as Bill Gates contends, digital technology will
pervade every corner of human existence, we must take time to analyze the effects
of the big 'e' on the business environment. It is a significant revolution: be it 'e-
commerce', 'e-business' or 'e-culture'. However, we believe the revolution is not
just about the high profile 'dot com' companies that have sprung up in this brave
new world. They will be found to be, as IBM's boss, Lou Gerstner, puts it, 'fire-flies
before the storm – all stirred up, throwing off sparks' (*The Economist*, 26 June 1999).
Gerstner believes that the real seismic business upheaval will occur when the big
players 'get wired'. Although Gerstner respects the progress made by the new
Internet star players such as Amazon.com, he points out that if, and when,
Wal-Mart become wired Amazon's fire-fly proportions will be apparent.

Even in 1999, at the height of Amazon's profile, IBM, with only 25 per cent of
its business being e-related, dwarfed Amazon's revenues, especially the profits.
Collectively by mid-1999, the top 25 Internet companies had generated close to $5
billion in revenues. IBM, not at that time a major Internet player, had generated
some $20 billion revenue through e-business.

the winners will be big *and* fast *and* clever

In mid-1999 Rupert Murdoch
declared that News Corporation would 'transform itself into an Internet company'
(*Guardian*, 2 July 1999). This was less than six months after he had declared that
the Internet was 'not the death-knell of the old'. Murdoch went further, adding
that no longer would big beat small but fast would beat slow. Others have argued
that in the Internet environment clever will beat big. Murdoch and the others will
be wrong, and Murdoch knows it. The winners will be big *and* fast *and* clever. What
is most likely to happen is that the financial and intellectual clout required to
utilize the Net for competitive advantage will stay with the 'super' companies.
Rather than levelling the playing field, the Net will further tilt it in favour of the
super league.

What Murdoch recognizes, like all good players, is the potential of the Internet
to destroy the current balance of power. As Michael Dell (the chairman of Dell
Computer) puts it, 'The Internet is like a weapon sitting on a table waiting to be
picked up by you or your competitors' (*Financial Times*, 26 August 1999). Dell
should know: Dell.com is the biggest e-business site on the Internet, with 43 per

cent of sales being generated and handled electronically. Dell expect that figure to hit 70 per cent in the near future. In March 1999 the *Financial Times* ran an electronic business special. Its headline was 'Competitors sharpen up their weapons for the digital contest'. Its message, like Andy Grove's, was that 'if a company of any size is not thinking of how the Internet can be used to make its business more efficient, its competitors undoubtedly are'. When the big players, like Wal-Mart, and News Corporation, transform themselves, that is when the real revolution will be truly unleashed. Senior executives intuitively know this is a 'when' not an 'if' issue. They know the environment is changing. A survey carried out by the Economist Intelligence Unit in 1999 (*see* Fig. 5.1) showed that a significant number of executives believe that by 2002 the Internet would have 'transformed' the global marketplace.

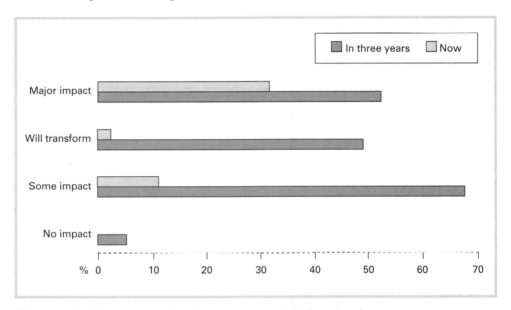

Figure 5.1   The impact of the Internet on the global marketplace
Sources: Economist Intelligence Unit and Booz Allen and Hamilton

Although this was true of executives worldwide, the picture in the UK was nowhere near as optimistic. Research commissioned by CISCO and ORACLE showed that British executives fall neatly into two categories – those who have ignored the e-revolution and those who are in its vanguard. Many British executives remain technophobes, prompting George Cox (Director General of the Institute of Directors) to say, 'that makes me very worried' (*Financial Times*, 29 September 1999). Given the lack of imagination of the average executive it is safe to assume that if *they* know it is coming then the revolution *is* coming.

What are the elements that will make up this environmental revolution? Clearly, the first element is the Internet. Most of the great technological shifts have occurred because of the desire to accelerate the exchange of information. Humans may have wanted to fly but the first commercial use of the plane was to deliver mail – to speed communication. The pony express, morse code, the telegraph, wireless and television all provided faster and faster communication channels. And then came the Internet. What initially held up the development of the World Wide Web was what was considered slow access and processing capabilities. Now that the hard and soft elements of the system, including the language, are in place and permitting almost instantaneous communication, the Internet will be unstoppable.

The first thing to recognize is the inevitable pervasiveness of the Internet. We are already in the Internet age. Andy Grove, the boss of Intel, has said that by 2005 'there won't be any "internet" companies' (*Sunday Times*, 12 September 1999). What he meant was the distinction will have ceased to be relevant. Just as we would not mention that a company used telephones to distinguish its techno-logical advantage so there will be no point mentioning that a company is 'wired'. It is estimated that by 2003 business-to-business electronic trade in the US will be close to $1.5 trillion. Business-to-consumer trade in the US will break $75 billion by 2002. In the UK the figures are more modest but growing. The Net has forced business-to-business institutions, such as the stock exchange, to overhaul completely their operations. As the Stock Exchange computer failure in April 2000 showed, such restructuring brings problems as well as advantages.

One advantage of the Internet is that it need not be resource intensive, which is one of the reasons that make business start-ups less of a problem with the Internet. Venture capital, for example, is actually searching for 'ideas'. Great companies from little garages really do grow (although it is still the case that, Internet or not, most new businesses fail – ideas without clout will not survive in the business environment). The power of the new technology is being exerted right across the business environment. The US e-commerce lead is the result, at least in part, of the extremely low incremental cost of Net access. Britain's high telephone charges, especially for local calls, mean that, on average, a British user will spend only 30 per cent of the time of an American on-line in any month. That is the equivalent of charging to go window shopping. Either the window shopping will stop or the charging will. Andy Grove believes the charging will stop as a result of competitive pressures. Technology has already created the possibility of both faster and cheaper access. Companies who cling to high-price strategies to more discerning customers will have to reassess or die. The evidence is that few companies relish the idea of death, so they will change

we are in the e-age and the business environment will never be the same

strategy. That will, in turn, generate the critical mass that will transform e-business from a fad into an institution. We are in the e-age and the business environment will never be the same.

One consequence of the new environment will be the inevitable changes in stated rules. Current corporate law was developed in the pre-Internet age and has difficulty coping with issues such as intellectual capital, liability and taxation as they are manifested in the cyber-world. The intellectual capital question – difficult at the best of times – has fallen into the equivalent of a cyberspace legal black hole. A European Parliamentary committee attempting to clarify the legal issues surrounding e-commerce has stated that there is:

A need for harmonized and unambiguous regulation at the European level, [the Hallyday case] exemplifies the very negative consequences that may arise from a confusion between these new, specific businesses of the information society and their approximate traditional counterparts, like printers or publishers.

The Hallyday case, to which the statement referred, was brought, successfully, by a French model, Estelle Hallyday, in 1999, against an Internet service provider for allowing her image to be posted on its websites. The significance of the case was that she sued the provider, not the person who posted the image. The French court therefore established equivalence, in France at least, between publishers and service providers. The quiltwork pattern of national laws within Europe will not hinder the speed of the development of Internet business, but it may distort that development in a manner disadvantageous to the European market. According to Forrester Research, Europe's Internet economy could be less than two-thirds of its potential by 2003. The creation of new laws needs to be sooner rather than later and perhaps the European Parliament might not be the best institution to achieve it. The laws should be both liberating and enforceable. Most importantly to the business player, they must be accounted for in the development of strategies and tactics in the 'e-conomy'.

Another consequence of the e-age will be structural. Ray Lane, the chairman of Oracle, believes that most chief executives of Fortune 500 companies are totally unaware and unprepared for the massive structural changes that will be inevitable if they are to survive. Vertically integrated structures are a recipe for inertia, Lane argues:

The whole balance sheet approach to accounting, the command and control structure of companies, where we have either the smartest or the most powerful persona at the top and vertically integrated structures between the CEO and the people who really have knowledge about what is really going on – that will disappear.

What will replace it, according to Lane, is a structure based on the possession of knowledge. Those who have it will 'become more powerful because they can act on it quicker and you don't need the command and control structure'. All Lane has done is to update the 'knowledge is power' dictum and replace it with 'knowledge plus speed of communication is power'.

This is also what the consultancy opportunists have identified as a major revenue generator. PricewaterhouseCoopers (PwC), for example, sell its Business Process Outsourcing (www.pwcglobal.com/bpo) product on the basis that what is of peripheral concern to the customer is PwC's core business. Their sales pitch is that outsourcing the customer's processes allows their 'management to focus on [their] core business – what [they] do best'. The way in which PwC is able to do that, they argue, is because 'the back office functions [the customer] may be considering as candidates for outsourcing are: finance and accounting; human resources; procurement; real estate; tax compliance; internal audit; applications process and maintenance'. Coincidentally, PwC point out that those precise functions are 'what we do best; they are our core business, where we excel'. In other words, there is a powerful and persuasive synergy between two core businesses. PwC has recognized the emergence, accelerated by the Internet, of what has been called the 'Hollywood effect'. This means that the 'boundaries of companies' will change. No longer will companies resemble the old Hollywood studios who employed and controlled everybody required to develop, make and distribute a film. In future they will resemble the new Hollywood studios who now assemble special teams and individuals to collaborate on specific projects to disband thereafter. Companies will become loose alliances of smaller firms and units. They will come together and remain together out of mutual needs and beliefs.

However, their disadvantage is that they can as easily be dismantled. Many organizations who outsourced a whole variety of functions have re-insourced (if there is such a word) those same functions. Security, for example, was never a sensible function to outsource and companies are beginning to realize as much. So if an organization intends to pursue the outsourcing approach it must make sure that the function to be outsourced is genuinely peripheral and not only apparently so. Making that distinction is time consuming and not cheap. Failing to do so is quicker, but far more expensive in the long term. Take one simple example. PwC cite accounting as a function they can outsource for you. Cisco, the Internet equipment maker, says that it is close to perfecting a system that will enable you to close your quarterly books two hours after the close of business at the end of each period. How? Because all its accounting data will be online. Why then hand over, and pay for, this function to PwC?

The new, electronically modified environment will have other consequences. It will throw up some strange bedfellows as new alliances are formed. Microsoft and

Ford, for example, have teamed up to promote personalized vehicle construction and delivery. Amazon have bought into Sotheby's, recognizing the success of eBay which had already allied itself with Butterfield and Butterfield, a traditional San Francisco auction house. Sega Enterprises embarked on a joint enterprise with Nomura Securities, which will enable Sega's Dreamcast console to be used to access Nomura's online brokerage activities. Perhaps most astonishingly, Ocean Fund International offered $3.6 billion for the eight Vegas and New Jersey casinos owned by Caesar's Palace. Ocean Fund is the owner of what is reputedly the Web's busiest site, sex.com, and the bid was virtually a cash bid. The large amounts of capital had been generated by pay-per-view hits at the sex.com site. Irrespective of the success or failure of the bid, it indicates a willingness by the new not to be swallowed by the old. The new companies have flagged their intentions to be aggressive acquirers of complementary businesses. The environment may have changed, but the game sounds the same.

The Internet will have unimagined consequences. The best players are those who can adapt to changing environmental conditions, whatever the cause. Atmosphere, mood and technology tend to be accorded insufficient importance in the development of organizational strategies. As with any of the characteristics of the game, neglecting the effect of the environment will be severely punished.

skill

how do we play?

Enhance yours, diminish theirs.

However motivated, aware of the opposition, knowledgeable of the rules and in tune with the environment players might be, if they do not possess the requisite *skill* set they will fail. This chapter deals with the skill set that players need to develop in order to be successful in the business game. The details of the skill set as described by our interviewees tended to vary, but one skill was agreed by them all – flexibility. Brendan O'Neill of ICI said it was the only essential skill. He described it as 'the ability to be able to adapt your behaviour, relative to the prevailing circumstances and other players, such that you achieve the greatest possible success'.

By skill we mean the ability to be able to deliver technique under pressure. While thousands of average footballers can competently pass a ball from A to B, how many can do so while running flat out, being lent on and kicked by another player, and can still deliver the ball at almost 90° to the running line? Not many, which is why David Beckham, David Ginola and Ryan Giggs are such sought-after players. They possess skills that transparently affect the success rate of their organizations. What we, as analysts, need to assess is the extent to which players' deficiencies prevent them from delivering their skills. Is Giggs injured too often? Is Beckham suspended too often? Are Ginola's defensive frailties too expensive? If, on balance, we decide that they are net contributors to the organizational effort then they must be retained and developed.

In the business game, just as in the sports game, there are a range of generic playing skills, or core capabilities in modern parlance. The list has no surprises: every organization wants workers, at all levels, who are team players, dynamic, customer-focused, outgoing, enthusiastic and service-oriented. That list was, incidentally, taken from a Costa Coffee advertisement for part-time counter staff. What we must do is analyze the buzzwords. We must unpick each concept in order to make sensible judgements about the utility and appropriateness of them all to the business player. What you, the reader, must do with this information, is relate it to your game and distinguish the skills you consider essential from those that are either merely desirable or just cosmetic.

So what skills do business players need? They must be:

- communicators
- propagandists
- politicians
- team players
- leaders
- knowledgeable
- lucky.

communication

Communication is the process by which we convey (and receive) information and knowledge to and from individuals or groups, usually in order to persuade them of the validity of our position. It is vital to understand the importance of receiving information as well as transmitting it. Good communicators are good listeners, good receivers. They are open to new ideas, they are sensitive to mood, hungry for knowledge. This is a practical, hard-nosed assessment, not a 'faddish' requirement. Being a good listener may or may not make you a wonderful human being, but it certainly makes you a more effective player. People will more willingly supply information to a good listener and information is the lifeblood of the effective game player.

The forms of communication are varied. They include verbal, written, facial, body language and semiotics. Semiology is the study of signals – how are signals sent and what is their purpose. Marketing and advertising are, perhaps, the most obvious business examples of semiology because they are centrally concerned with more subliminal signalling than other aspects of the business game. Just think about toy advertising strategies. While the actual target is the parent, the initial pressure is exerted on the children, who redirects it to the parent. 'What sort of a parent are you', advertisers subliminally ask, 'that you would allow your child to be disadvantaged in the eyes of the other children?' A powerful signal.

The most important factor in communication is an interest in people. Some people are simply fascinated by other human beings. As a result of their own need to interact they will develop communication skills that facilitate such interaction. In games that require a high level of communication skills, look for players who are interested in others.

in games that require a high level of communication skills, look for players who are interested in others

propaganda

What we often want from the business player, however, is not straight communication but communication for competitive advantage. What this entails is conscious packaging of the message. 'Propaganda' accurately describes the activity of message packaging. Language is precisely chosen and carefully packaged and the injection of those packaged messages into the communication process has a powerful effect on the consciousness of recipients. The good propagandists are, therefore, very precise about language – it is the primary tool of their trade. Watching the mouthpieces of the rail operators packaging and repackaging their messages in the wake of the Paddington carnage was something of a master-class in the art of spinning.

One of the acknowledged masters of spin, Charlie Whelan, described it as the art of the 'palatable'. In May 1999 Marks & Spencer's chief executive, Peter Salsbury, made the following comment after announcing his company's dreadful slump in profits: 'We have been identifying what went wrong and starting to put it right. We are pretty confident now and we would hope to see some improvement in the coming months' (*Evening Standard*, 18 May 1999). Never mind the quality, feel the tone. Salsbury's was perfectly crafted to allay fear without promising anything of substance. What Salsbury chose not to mention were the actual figures. They showed that Salsbury's statement was accurate – there was an improving trend – but there were still massive problems. The job of his messages at that time was to reassure, it was tone not content that was important. Knowing the objective of your communication is as important as the method of delivering it. Content and form must be compatible in order to provide maximum impact.

Language has enormous power not only on a corporate but also on an individual level. Research has shown, for example, that clever, witty interventions by individuals at meetings are viewed by others as denoting effectiveness and intelligence. Pfeffer and Sutton (1999) go so far as to say that 'appearing smart is mostly accomplished by sounding smart; being confident, articulate, eloquent, and filled with interesting information and ideas: and having a good vocabulary'. The problem with this, according to the authors, is that 'smart talk is confused with performance'. The phrase, 'they talk a good game', comes to mind. We argue that it is the organization and the others who have a problem, not the intervenor. The person whose interventions are actually seen as performance is playing an effective game and will continue to play it for as long as it succeeds.

The mystification of language has always played a powerful role in the establishment of status. Once you codify language in abstract terms there is always the need to de-codify it to make it real again. For example, the language of the law is so complex that judges are constantly required to explain judgements using language that is understandable. In a fascinating article in the *American Business Law Journal*, Archer and Cohen (1998) maintain that judicial opinions remain obscure if judges use inappropriate metaphors to explain their decisions. In other words their explanations are no clearer because the explanatory language they use is just as jargon-laden as that which they seek to clarify. What the successful business game players must understand is firstly how powerful metaphors and analogies can be in explaining concepts, but secondly that inappropriate use of metaphors can be just as powerful negatively. The problem is that all games have their own language and business is no exception. An integral part of knowing any business is knowing its language, because the language will contain its codes. The skill of the propagandists, whether they are in marketing, advertising or strategy, is to recognize the power of the communication process and to use it. They must intuitively be able to encode and decode in the language of the game. The expert propagandist is, therefore, a tactically adept, competitively focused communicator.

political skills

When these super communicators start to play and to use their linguistic skills their political skills are also revealed. Politics is the art of getting what you want. Political skills are universal – they include being able to develop trust, knowledge of the game, being able to influence, negotiate, bluff, hold your nerve and deceive. Jane Clarke, a director of a business psychology consultancy, has written about 'office politics' (1999). As she points out, office politics must not be taken lightly, especially in the boardroom. The people who aspire to 'serve' on the board are those with enormous egos and a matching single-mindedness and drive. They are expert at 'handling' people and events. However, when they come together as a board they are confronted not by compliant subordinates but by equals. They will, therefore, need to possess skills in alliance building, they need to be able to network, provide favours, and be able either to move closer or distance themselves relative to events. Most importantly, and rarely acknowledged, they must enjoy exercising power. They must actually welcome the responsibilities, opportunities and problems associated with power. It is almost taboo to admit that 'I want to run everything', but that is why most people are in positions of power. The problem is that power can corrupt. When John Prescott went into politics, did he really do it in order to be driven 100 yards in a ministry car? Almost certainly not, but that is where it led.

Returning to the board, the problem is that 10 or 20 members may all wish to be the chairman or CEO. Consequently, personality clashes, friendships and favours will fashion the political atmosphere. Generally in both boards and governmental cabinets there is a notion of collective responsibility (*see* Brady, 1999). However, each board member also has a functional responsibility such as finance, marketing, sales and operations. Success in politics therefore depends on a delicate mixture of personality, knowledge, function and allies. Unless all factors are present then success is unlikely. Without the clout of a major department, for example, your

without knowledge of the game you will be excluded; without allies you will be isolated

voice will be ignored; without knowledge of the game you will be excluded; without allies you will be isolated; without the appropriate personality you will be disregarded. Business politicians also need to be constantly developing each factor. For example, if they are in weak departments they must either try to get to a strong department or work to make their weak department stronger.

An important aspect of power is that it is relative. Knowledge of the political game is knowledge of the relativity of power. That relativity is not only in terms of status, but also of domain and issue. Who is more powerful, Bill Gates or Tony Blair, Tiger Woods or Alex Ferguson? It depends on the time, the place and the issue. Power is not always, in fact not often, coercive. Most often it is the result of influence, compromise, negotiation, sympathy and empathy. A common definition of power is when A gets B to undertake an action that B would not otherwise have done. For us this is still too coercive. Our definition of power is the ability of A to get B to undertake an action B always wanted to do but never actually knew it.

However, politics is not simply about the advancement of self within an organization. It is about getting what you want, as an individual or a group. If you are Mother Teresa or Mahatma Gandhi you might use your political skills for the benefit of others; if you do not wish to run everything you will use your skills to remain anonymous. If your skills are inadequate you will not get what you want. As Thelma said in in the movie *Thelma and Louise*, 'You get what you settle for.' A failure to recognize the significance of the political game, either intra- or inter-organizational, is a huge skill deficit. Effectively you are competing in a game you do not even know is being played.

team playing

Much has been written about the importance of team work in the corporate world. A team is where the whole is *greater* than the sum of the parts. A 'work-group' is where the whole is *only* the sum of the parts. So what do we mean by team players? Is it those prepared to subordinate themselves for the good of the team? Is it those prepared to run the team? Is it those who are innovative, creative, supportive, deferential, leaders or followers? Team players can be all of these things.

The single most important indicator of team success is balance. Balance is more than simple complementarity. In the wake of a management shake-up at Sainsbury's in October 1999, their Chairman, Sir George Bull, said that Dino Adriano (Group Strategy) and David Bremner 'would make an excellent team' (*Financial Times*, 14 October 1999). What he meant was that their abilities were complementary. This is not the same as saying they constitute a balanced team; in fact, the functional power they respectively wielded had changed hands.

> competitive advantage is gained through an ability to spot a balanced team when it emerges and then to nurture its members

So balance is rather that intangible cocktail of necessary skills and personalities that great teams have. Unfortunately, while good managers can recognize a balanced team when it appears, it is almost impossible to create such a balance. This does not, of course, mean it should not be tried, because it is through the process of trying that good teams will emerge. Competitive advantage is gained through an ability to spot a balanced team when it emerges and then to nurture its members and carefully replace them at the most effective moment. The policy at Juventus under Marcello Lippi ruthlessly applied this strategy on an annual basis. Lippi relied on a solid foundation of tried-and-trusted players, plus the introduction of superstar performers in key roles.

How can this approach be applied to the more mundane surroundings of most jobs? While the star players may be enjoying the game, most ordinary workers probably will not be. How can such workers be motivated to continue to perform at a competent level? This is just one of the issues that are the concern of the team leader. And it is even more concerning for those responsible for work groups. A common mistake currently afflicting the business world is the assumption that any loose grouping of people should be designated, and, therefore, treated as a team. One of the best ways of ascertaining the existence of a team is to ask the players whether they believe they are part of one. If there is any doubt, they are either not in a team or in an unsuccessful one.

leadership

There is a continual stream of business books that extol the virtues of military and sports heroes and even orchestra leaders. They are the 'inspiration for business leaders on how to achieve truly outstanding team performance' (Jonassen, 1999). Although it can be useful to apply analogous situations such as the military to leadership, it is counter-productive to see the military, for example, as a perfectly transferable model. What is helpful is to identify the generic principles of leadership. Leaders are, for example, team players in the sense that without people to lead they cannot exist. However, the language of leadership often distances the leader and the team. This misses the point of great leadership, since one of the essential skills of effective leadership is the ability to be simultaneously part of, and apparently separate from, the team as the situation demands.

A list of qualities required of effective leaders would look very much like that which we have suggested for all business players – good communicators, focused, politician, high technical skills and strong cognitive abilities. What differentiates leaders from other players? First, we cannot ignore the power issue. Leaders enjoy exercising power. Leaders do not surprisingly emerge from the ranks. They covet power, seek it and welcome its pressures. They put themselves in positions to be able to bid for power and/or accept it. Whatever bosses might say to the contrary, they usually want to be the boss. Bosses are driven to achieve simply for the sake of achieving. They are not primarily driven by salaries or comfort, but by achievement.

Another quality leaders need is a 'feel' for the game. They need not necessarily be the best players but they must either be, or have been, players. Whilst being a player is not inherently necessary to leadership, it is perceived by those being led as essential. Without 'street-cred' the exercise of leadership becomes extremely difficult. So leaders will tend to have been ex-players, ex-musicians and ex-workers, although not necessarily the best at their game. Where their skills lie is in the leadership task itself.

The problem of identifying generic leadership skills is clear if you look at the variety of successful leadership styles that exist. What are the generic skills exemplified by Alex Ferguson and Arsene Wenger, by Tony Blair and Margaret Thatcher, by Pattern and Montgomery, Hitler and Ghandi? It would be difficult to find a more diverse group, and yet they all got people to follow them. The key factor of leadership is appropriateness: what is appropriate in war may not be so in peace; what is right for the delicate negotiations of a merger may not be right for the turnarounds necessary in a failing organization; what is right in a start-up may not be right in a consolidation. This is why personal style and situation are intrinsically complementary indicators of leadership potential.

In recent years the significant skills that enable leaders to adopt different, and, therefore, appropriate styles, have been given the generic term 'emotional intelligence' (EI) (Goleman, 1995). By emotional intelligence Goleman means competencies such as the ability to work with others. Effective leaders are alike in one crucial way – they all have a high degree of emotional intelligence. However, IQ and technical skills are not irrelevant. They do matter, but mainly as 'threshold capabilities; that is, they are entry-level requirements for executive positions'. Goleman concludes, 'My research, along with other recent studies, clearly shows that emotional intelligence is the *sine qua non* of leadership.' His research also reveals significant correlations between EI and strong corporate performance. EI is also not simply the prerogative of the quiet, 'sensitive' leader. The blusterers and shouters must also possess it to be successful – provided that blustering and shouting are appropriate to the situation. EI helps you decide issues of appropriateness. EI is also an essential component of aggressive play. The mind games played by all sports people is simply not possible without a high degree of EI. Being able to empathize, for example, is vital in knowing how to irritate and tease an opponent. EI is, therefore, not only a passive skill.

> effective leaders are alike in one crucial way – they all have a high degree of emotional intelligence

Goleman provides a useful checklist of what he calls the components of EI at work:

- *Self-awareness* is the quality most often undervalued. The ability to recognize personal limitations is crucial. It doubly increases efficiency because you will be able to devolve more effectively and not waste time attempting tasks that are beyond you.

- *Self-regulation* is the implementation mechanism for self-awareness. It 'frees us from being prisoners of our feelings'. It is the ability to be able to dwell for a split second before reacting – the old ploy of counting to ten. This does not mean never exploding, it means exploding having considered its effect.

- *Self-motivation* drives the leader and inspires the led. The self-motivated continually stretch themselves and, by association, those around them.

- *Empathy* refers to the extremely difficult practice of putting yourself in someone else's shoes – and actually caring about what it is like to be in those shoes. Empathy is a key coaching skill. The really good leader will almost certainly be a great coach of coaches.

- *Social skill* is 'the knack of finding common ground with people of all kinds – a knack for building rapport'. It is important to treat social skills as separate from the other components, even thought they will often be synonymous. The socially skilled leader will use those skills around the coffee machine, in the bar, in sports, in fact in any situation where colleagues are present. 'Social skill' is the ability to be able to utilize the other components of EI.

A clear example of appropriate leadership was General Colin Powell during the Gulf War. He perfectly complemented the style of his operations chief Norman Schwarzkopf. Powell has developed a set of 18 guidelines for appropriate leadership:

- Being responsible sometimes means getting people angry.

- The day soldiers stop bringing you their problems is the day you have stopped leading them. They have either lost confidence that you can help them or concluded that you do not care. Either case is a failure of leadership.

- Don't be buffaloed by experts and elites. Experts often possess more data than judgement. Elites can become so inbred that they produce haemophiliacs who bleed to death as soon as they are nicked in the real world.

- Don't be afraid to challenge the pros even in their own backyard.

- Never neglect details. When everyone's mind is dulled or distracted the leader must be doubly vigilant.

- You don't know what you can get away with until you try.

- Keep looking below surface appearances. Don't shrink from doing so just because you might not like what you find.

- Organization doesn't really accomplish anything. Plans don't accomplish anything either. Theories of management don't much matter. Endeavours succeed or fail because of the people involved. Only by attracting the best people will you accomplish great deeds.

- Organization charts and fancy titles count for next to nothing.

- Never let your ego get so close to your position that when your position goes, your ego goes with it.

- Fit no stereotypes. Don't chase the latest management fads. The situation dictates which approach best accomplishes the team's mission.

- Perpetual optimism is a force multiplier.

- 'Powell's rules for picking people': look for intelligence and judgement and, most critically, a capacity to anticipate, to see around corners. Also look for loyalty, integrity, a high-energy drive, a balanced ego and the drive to get things done. Select quality not qualifications.

- Great leaders are almost always great simplifiers, who can cut through argument, debate and doubt, to offer a solution everybody can understand [borrowed by Powell from Michael Korda].

- Use the formula P40 to 70, in which P stands for the probability of success and the numbers indicate the percentage of information acquired. Once the information is in the 40 to 70 range, go with your gut.

- The commander in the field is always right and the rear echelon is wrong, unless proved otherwise.

- Have fun in your command. Don't always run at a breakneck pace. Take leave when you've earned it. Spend time with your families.

- Command is lonely.

technical expertise

In addition to the emotional intelligence needed by all players, and especially leaders, there must also be technical expertise. This is gained by a combination of methods that include both experience and education, theory and practice. These are the 'threshold capabilities' of which Goleman speaks. All the other skills are irrelevant if you cannot actually kick the ball, analyze foreign office briefs, understand tank warfare or read a shareholder report. Entry qualifications cannot necessarily be learned. Gender, for example, can be the most important qualification necessary for entry into some games; so can race, religion, sexual orientation, or disability. These are games controlled by the bigoted. The same principles apply to so-called 'glass ceilings' which bar people on a variety of grounds. Exclusivity is still rampant in the professions where even the language is constructed to exclude the majority of the population.

If you are not barred in any serious way then your entry qualifications will normally be judged on technical skills, such as business planning and budgetary control, and on cognitive abilities, such as analytical powers. The contemporary business environment also needs more competence in 'fluid intelligence' than in 'crystallized intelligence'. Using the water analogy devised by the British psychologist Raymond Cattell (1987), the distinction is between fluidity (able to take any shape) and crystallization (as inflexible as ice crystals). In modern organizational environments, fluid intelligence is 'on-the-spot reasoning ability, a skill not basically dependent on our experience'. Companies encounter problems when trying to promote employees with essentially 'crystallized intelligence' into positions requiring 'fluid intelligence'. Ally 'fluid intelligence' to other cognitive abilities, mix in some emotional intelligence and add Colin Powell's leadership lessons, and you have almost the complete range of skills necessary to be a competent business player.

luck

There is one skill element to add – luck. When asked which quality he most desired in his generals, Napoleon is reported to have answered 'Luck'. If luck actually exists then the trick is to simply recognize those who have it and appoint them to decision-making jobs in your organization. But we suspect there is no such thing as luck; what is actually happening is opportunism. Lucky people are those who recognize random opportunities and seize them. It is not luck that won the European Cup for Manchester United, but their ability to apply pressure in the opposition penalty area was sufficient to amplify the odds in their own favour. This does not, of course, guarantee success but it alters the odds in your favour. Similarly, insider knowledge of trading intentions distorts the odds. It is important that rearranging the odds does not damage the game – if it does then it will be outlawed.

Gemplus is one of the leading manufacturers of smartcards in the world. The French company, founded by Marc Lassus, a 40-something French physicist, now has deals with industry giants Microsoft, Deutsche Telecom, Dell and Compaq. Was this the result of superb planning or luck? Neither, claims Marc Lassus. 'I could sit back and tell you everything was completely planned. But I have to be honest – we haven't planned very much of this, and to some extent we still don't. We have just learned to be opportunistic.' What this statement demonstrates is the need to plan on two levels: the rational and the random. Good players will plan for the expected, but will also plan to be flexible and adaptable enough to seize the opportunities provided by the random. As Gary Player once famously said, 'The more I practise, the luckier I get.' When Terry Venables handed that vital penalty kick to Gareth Southgate in Euro 1996 the result was not bad luck but bad preparation. Southgate had only taken one previous senior-level penalty, and missed it. Better preparation may not, ultimately, have resulted in victory, but it would have altered the odds. In business altering the odds is euphemistically referred to as 'creating competitive advantage'.

If, then, playing the business game is simply about utilizing the skills outlined in this chapter, why do players fail? Because they fail to exercise those skills. In particular, according to *Fortune* (21 June, 1999), the problem is with 'bad execution'. In an article entitled 'Why CEOs Fail', the authors argue that the single consistent factor in CEO failure is rarely strategy, internal politics or anything so grand – although all may contribute – it is failure to implement, 'not getting things done, being indecisive, not delivering on commitments'. The skill set we have advocated in this chapter is aimed at this simple but apparently dull task. Successful players must keep in mind that failure to implement grand ideas only leads to failure.

part 3

winning

Be clear about what constitutes success for *you* and pursue it. Don't alter your goal mid-stream. When you achieve success, reset your targets and pursue them.

Part 3 is about how to win the game. To be accurate, we should talk about success rather than victory because, as we have already identified, the games we play need not be competitive in their structure. Being successful requires that players concern themselves with three distinct but interrelated activities – *knowing*, *coaching* and *exploiting*. They need to know as much as possible about each of the MORES factors that we have established constitute the fabric of any game. With that knowledge they must be able to construct a coaching plan that will educate themselves and other relevant players in the techniques and skills that are necessary for participation. Finally, they must be tactically and technically adroit enough to be able to identify and exploit opportunities as they are thrown up during the course of the game. Successful game players, therefore, achieve their success in one of two ways: they either play the game very well as it exists, or they change the nature of the game to one in which they are able to play very well. They exploit their knowledge and coaching to achieve maximum success.

knowing

what do we need to know?

Knowledge is *potential* power. You must target it, capture it, protect it and use it in order to release that potential.

In March 1999 Bill Gates, addressing an audience at the London Business School, declared that the Internet will change business practices so dramatically that 'everyone will be a knowledge worker'. Nearly 30 years earlier the former chairman of CITICORP, Walter Wriston, made an equally dramatic statement. He said that banking was not about money, it was 'about information'. Both men agreed that it was information that provides the real competitive advantage. They also agreed that the information revolution, in which we find ourselves, is unprecedented. But the management guru Peter F. Drucker, said their claim was 'absolute nonsense' (1999). Drucker, also a historian, argues that the societal effects of the Gutenberg-inspired information revolution of the mid-fifteenth century were as dramatic as those we are currently encountering.

Drucker also contends that the revolution has not yet actually arrived – and is being delayed – because we misunderstand the nature of information. Where the revolutionary technologies have had most effect, for example, has been at the operational level. So the speed with which data has been able to be processed has put accounting and finance details at the fingertips of CEOs. But what the revolutionary processing power has not been able to provide is any assistance with the decisions that will be based upon the data. Decision making is based on analysis, and data collection and representation is not analysis. As Drucker states:

Neither preservation of assets nor cost control are senior management tasks. They are *operational tasks*. A serious cost disadvantage may indeed destroy a business. But business success is based on something totally different, the creation of value and wealth. This requires risk-taking decisions: on the theory of business, on business strategy, on abandoning the old and devising the new, on the balance between immediate profitability and market share. These decisions are the true senior management tasks.

We disagree with Drucker about the impact of this most recent information revolution on management tasks. We argue that increased technological power will fuel the development of business training facilities which will, in turn, provide decision makers with increased knowledge about the decision-making process. The next generation of business simulation software will be aimed precisely at this target. The authors are co-operating with Elixir-Studios (http://www.elixir-studios.com), a software game-design firm, in the development of a virtual reality game that will revolutionize education in the decision-making processes. Drucker says that with virtual reality surgeons can carry out 'virtual operations' whose outcomes may include 'virtually killing' patients. Then why not virtual business decision-making scenarios where 'virtual' mergers can win or lose 'virtual' millions? This will form the basis of coaching when the convergence of the market and supply of information – which Drucker also predicts – has occurred.

While the medium of delivery may be revolutionized, the purpose of that delivery remains the same – the provision of information as the key resource for knowledge development. This is why initiatives such as KPMG's 'High Performance Company', which talk impressively about 'info-structures', are missing the point. KMPG uses the Formula-One racing car as an analogy for businesses. The high performance company, they argue, is 'like a Formula-One racing car. It moves at speed. It is in a potentially dangerous environment. Success depends on multiple data feeds from sensors throughout the car, filtered through to the driver and the team in the pits.' The

knowledge is how you use information in the game situation: knowledge is information under pressure

problem is that the KMPG solution is to prioritize the car (the business structures) and not the people. The competitive advantage in Formula One is the driver. Ferrari have only become competitive because of Michael Schumacher. If Schumacher and Haakinnen switched cars everybody knows who would win. We agree with KPMG that the business environment is fast changing and potentially dangerous and that all businesses should aim to be like the best cars, but in a sense that is what already happens. The cars (businesses) as structures are relatively indistinguishable – it is the drivers who make them different.

The distinction between information and knowledge is similar to that we made between technique and skill. Skill is how you utilize technique in the game situation: skill is technique under pressure. Knowledge is how you use information in the game situation: knowledge is information under pressure. As a corporate resource, knowledge has always been the key differentiator. Having information that a short-cut exists and further information that the rules do not preclude its use gives a racer competitive knowledge from which to make tactical decisions. Intuitively we know that in situations such as a race or a game knowledge is power.

Although the business world talks about knowledge as a product, it is a uniquely intangible product. It is not something that can be acquired and then stored for use because some of it has only a limited life-span. Knowledge, as opposed to information, is dynamic. The knowledge transformation cycle has traditionally been depicted as in Fig. 7.1. In this model, data are seen as facts and statistics presented in their raw state without any accompanying analysis or context. Data are transformed into information when they have been subjected to analysis and categorization and subsequently summarized and placed in context. Information is transformed into knowledge when it is used to identify connections, comparisons and, most importantly when it has been subjected to criticism. Knowledge is information transformed by experience, judgement, intuition, values and perception. It is at that point that the accomplished learners (or learning organizations) turn their attention to the collection of more data in order to reinvigorate the knowledge cycle. By comparison with such a system those like the KPMG product are little more than state-of-the-art filing and dissemination systems.

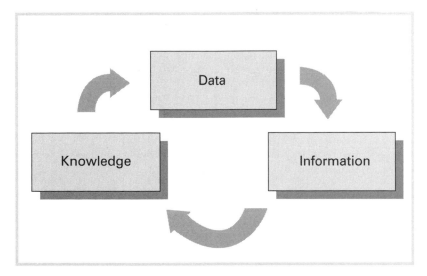

Figure 7.1 The knowledge transformation cycle

The problem with knowledge is its predominantly tacit nature. It is, of course, not possible to make explicit all that is tacit because the very nature of tacit knowledge is intuitive and experiential. Nevertheless, it is possible to make explicit knowledge that is hoarded by its owners. This is precisely what the old craft apprenticeship schemes were designed to do. Apprenticeships are a formalized variant of what Nonaka and Takeuchi call socialization (1995). The process of transferring tacit knowledge to others converts it to explicit knowledge. Apprenticeships do this by forcing the knowledge holders to be knowledge sharers and allowing someone else to observe and listen. Socialization achieves the same effect by more subtle, and sometimes less effective, means. The role of the knowledge manager, therefore, is to identify those with tacit knowledge valuable to the organization and then to put in place organizational mechanisms that aid the process of sharing.

Of course, barriers can prevent the effective management of knowledge. One is that tacit knowledge is very often undervalued as unscientific, anecdotal and insubstantial by those who are more comfortable with explicitly codified working environments. Individuals and groups are reluctant to share because they view knowledge as a zero-sum game in which the act of giving away knowledge somehow diminishes them as an individual or group. According to a survey conducted by Huseman and Goodman (1999) 78 per cent of major US companies who responded claimed that they were attempting to become 'knowledge-based'. However, the authors believed that the majority of that 78 per cent were actually 'nowhere near' achieving their goal. Primarily the failure can be attributed to a spectacular lack of knowledge about knowledge. In its simplest terms, knowledge is the transformation of information under the pressure of the game. The game activates the information.

What actions can players take that will make them knowledge players – not hard workers but smart players? There are four aspects of that knowledge ownership that all players must understand (*see* Fig. 7.2) – how to get it (*capture*), how to keep it (*security*), how to harness it (*management*) and how to use it (*operations*).

capture

If knowledge is transformed information, then capturing knowledge is literally impossible; unless, that is, you can capture the resource that transformed the information into knowledge in the first place – the human being. Hence the prevalence of head-hunting, which is knowledge capture at its most pure. This does assume, of course, that the head-hunted will share their knowledge with others in the corporation when they arrive. Notwithstanding the intractability of capturing pure knowledge, organizations must still try to do so. This section on knowledge capture addresses the issues that surround the targeting and acquisition of

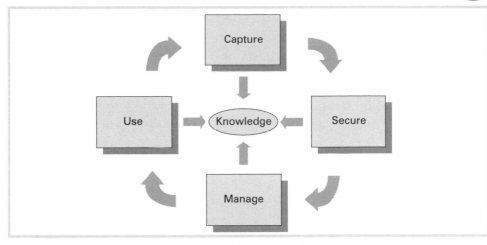

Figure 7.2 The four aspects of knowledge ownership

information in your own organization and the organizations in your game. It is about the competitive intelligence that players require in order to play effectively. This process of intelligence gathering is focused internally as well as externally. Organizations without knowledge of themselves are as blind as those without knowledge of the other players. For the remainder of the book we will refer only to 'intelligence' and not 'competitive intelligence' – any intelligence exists to create competitive advantage.

There are four sub-sections to knowledge capture. First, *why* do we need intelligence – what is the case for business intelligence at all? Second, we will provide some *definitions* of concepts, which we believe are necessary because of the confusion that surrounds the intelligence function. Third, we will examine *how* the intelligence function is practised. Finally, we will identify the *problems* that organizations encounter when they attempt to capture intelligence. We argue throughout for the primacy of the analyst, not least because the role of intelligence is to aid the decision-making process and decision making is an intensely human activity.

> organizations without knowledge of themselves are as blind as those without knowledge of the other players

Traditionally the route to knowledge has been presented as a hierarchy that converts data (a raw number, for example) into information (that raw number presented in context, for example, a graph). Information is then converted into knowledge (information transformed by analysis), which is, in turn, converted into wisdom (knowledge placed in an experiential context). However, for the intelligence specialist there is no such thing as raw data because the very act of targeting contextualizes data. This automatically converts data into information. For the intelligence worker, therefore, the search for knowledge begins with information. Knowledge remains in the same positional relationship as in the knowledge hierarchy – it is information transformed by contextual analysis. Finally, intelligence itself is defined as knowledge disseminated for a reason. The reason being, of course, that the 'targeters' have targeted it. Thus the act of targeting, and consequently the analytical input at every stage, is inherent in the intelligence process and means that the *intelligence cycle* is as shown in Fig. 7.3.

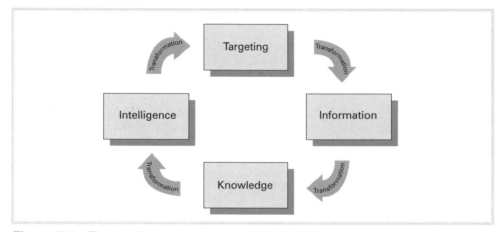

Figure 7.3 The intelligence cycle

why do we need intelligence?

Organizations need good intelligence to remain competitive. More than half of the Fortune 500 group of companies have a formalized intelligence input into their business strategies and it is safe to assume that there is some sort of intelligence input in all the companies, be it formal or informal. The advantage of formalization is that it can be adjusted and fine-tuned in response to its success, or otherwise, and consequently it can be more effective. Informal intelligence input is often isolated and, as a consequence, lost. Effective intelligence can help an organization to avoid failure. It provides the information resources necessary to anticipate the consequences of a rapidly changing environment, to respond to new or proliferating competition, and to re-orient strategy. Good intelligence can help to avoid surprise – in business there is no such thing as a 'pleasant' surprise.

The idea that intelligence is the most significant factor in inter-organizational rivalry is ancient. Over 2000 years ago the Chinese warrior/philosopher, Sun Tzu, wrote *The Art of War*, of which *Newsweek* once said, 'Absorb this book and you can throw out all those contemporary books about management leadership'. In *The Art of War* Sun Tzu argues that 'to fail to know the conditions of opponents because of a reluctance to give rewards for intelligence is ... uncharacteristic of a victorious chief'. In other words, it is stupid. He also said that 'what enables an intelligent government to overcome others ... is foreknowledge'. Sun Tzu added that foreknowledge 'can only be obtained from people, people who know the conditions of the enemy'. Consequently, the crucial elements of a competitive organization are a culture that awards a high status to intelligence (hence Sun Tzu's rewards) and a clear understanding that information is a people-oriented commodity. Intelligence is a commodity that is inherently valuable and consequently needs to be expertly managed for the benefit of the organization.

Although the underlying principles of intelligence are self-evidently ancient, the modern environment in which the profession is practised has changed significantly. First, in the post-industrial era knowledge has become much more of a commodity in itself; it both supports the intelligence process and is simultaneously its product. Second, communications technology has enabled new patterns and locations of work that are more knowledge-dependent than previously. Third, middle management, which traditionally acted as a conduit for knowledge transference around an organization, has been flattened out of the system. Fourth, the business dynamic has simply gathered pace at an extraordinary rate. This has, for example, enabled extremely narrow markets to be identified, targeted and exploited before competitors can react – unless, of course, they have the same information resources.

> although the principles of intelligence are ancient, the modern environment in which the profession is practised has changed significantly

Business players therefore need intelligence for both ancient and modern reasons. They also need to formalize it because, although it is estimated that over 90 per cent of information required by an organization is open source and easily available, more than 80 per cent is not held in formal corporate information systems – either because they do not exist or because they are not used. Instead informally gathered information is stored in personal filing systems, or most often in people's heads. Information held in this haphazard way cannot be integrated and consequently cannot be fully utilized.

what is intelligence?

What precisely is intelligence – what should it do and what value should it add? Intelligence analysts have defined strategic intelligence as: 'the use of behavioural information gathered on your competitors from primary sources to form the foundation for management decision making'. This is an interesting but limited definition. It focuses on behaviour and ignores intent. It implies that you should beware of current competitors but ignores potential competitors. It refers only to primary sources and not all sources. It speaks of management decision making and not all decision making. We suggest a simpler but more inclusive definition: 'the process of monitoring and manipulating the competitive environment'.

The notion of targeting is implicit in this definition. What is significant about sensible targeting is that it aims to provide optimum information, knowing just enough to make a decision. Too little or too much can cause indecision. A way of identifying what is significant is by locating information at the appropriate level of the intelligence function within an organization. There are three basic levels: *strategic, tactical* and *counter* intelligence. By strategic we mean board level – the level at which the analysis of the environment in which the organization operates forms an integral element of the policy process. Tactical refers to the managerial level where information is required that is specific to the current situation and to operational issues. At this level the managers need to be able to make decisions that deal with the here and now, and with the implementation of policies generated at the strategic level. Counter intelligence is primarily the province of the intelligence specialists and is concerned with defending the organization. In order that the organization can function effectively the various levels have to be integrated to create a simple, dynamic intelligence cycle that continuously feeds the corporate memory:

● *Target*: ask questions such as what should we gather, why should we gather it, how will we use it? The targeting must be appropriate: key questions need to be defined, the research process must be planned, and it must be able to deal with situations both actively (strategic) and reactively (crisis).

● *Collect*: gather the information by the most appropriate means. ELINT (electronic intelligence – monitoring an organization's activities), SIGINT (signal intelligence – monitoring an organization's communication traffic), and HUMINT (human intelligence – monitoring the organization in its entirety) are the three strands of successful intelligence collection.

● *Process*: verify (how good is the source, for example), evaluate, analyze (create knowledge), and integrate (feed the knowledge into the 'infostructure').

● *Use*: disseminate the product to the user, who will then re-direct the system in the light of the feedback and continue the dynamic of the cycle.

At any stage, information can be extracted from or fed back into the cycle in order to refresh and enhance the corporate memory.

best practices

What would this process look like in practice? What are the intelligence practices currently being employed and what are the problems currently being encountered? In other words, how is the business environment being monitored? Companies are putting in place a whole variety of mechanisms that pose as intelligence efforts – including surveillance on their own staff – but without the necessary culture of sharing in place these efforts will come to nothing. Procedures aimed at capturing information such as data mining, policy analysis and the establishment of knowledge centres are only able to add value if they represent the underlying ethos of the organization. In most instances this simply is not the case.

In November 1999 the BBC aired a programme that showed Tino Adriano, the then head of Sainsbury's supermarket operations, spending time actually working in his supermarkets in order to familiarize himself with the problems of his staff. One of the things Adriano uncovered was that the 'shoppers' trolleys', that is the slightly smaller trolleys, were the most popular with customers and that there were never sufficient to satisfy customer needs.

> procedures and structures have to be set in place that enable feedback and communication to occur naturally

When Adriano reported this to his management team he said, 'I didn't know about this', and proceeded to make arrangements to order more trolleys. This is a classic error of most management when they uncover a problem – they treat the symptom not the disease. The real question he should have asked was, 'Why didn't I know about this, and more to the point, why didn't you know about this?' As Adriano pointed out later in his talk, 'It's all about communication, we all need feedback.' We do, but it will not happen of its own accord. Procedures and structures have to be set in place that enable feedback and communication to occur naturally. If an organization is to nurture and value the intelligence function it must be a natural resultant of its culture, it cannot simply be grafted on. If the culture is not conducive to the intelligence process then what must happen, in the first instance, is that the climate must be altered in order to kick-start a cultural change.

We define climate as the everyday working environment and events that the personnel see around them – simple things like the standard operating procedures (SOPs), working practices and general behaviour of the management. A change of climate in favour of an intelligence-friendly organization entails changing from practices and behaviour that reward secrecy and hoarding information to those that reward sharing and disseminating information. In Sainsbury's, for example, staff on the night shift were actually forbidden to talk to each other while shelf stacking. How could they possibly exchange ideas of best practice in such an environment? Again, Adriano was astonished. Again he altered the practice, but not the culture that had generated the rule in the first place. Perhaps the fact that Adriano was moved upstairs shortly before the film was aired shows that Sainsbury's are belatedly recognizing the problem. It is not easy to develop transparent and sharing cultures, especially in the British context where we venerate secrecy. It may not be easy, but it is an essential prerequisite for organizational success.

If organizations can manage to free up the climate, and eventually the culture, they will find that the vast majority of the information they require is already in the system. As a consequence the collection process resembles windfall apple gathering rather than apple picking. You still have to be selective, but the donkey-work has been largely eliminated. Look at the efficiency of the 'grapevine'. Not only does the grapevine disseminate information at the speed of light, it also finds it in the first place. The establishment of coffee shops and other socialization areas do not merely provide refreshment and comfort, they also provide a sanctuary where information can be freely exchanged. It is in such places that the telephonists, receptionists, PAs and others with the real knowledge of the whole organization can mix openly with management. It is the place where those who know everything meet.

One of the most successful terrorist groups of the 1990s was the Peruvian Maoist, group, the Sendero Luminosa. The majority of its intelligence came from its network of 'agents' who were the ice-cream and newspaper sellers of the capital, Lima. They were on every corner and listened to every leisure conversation – they knew everything. Companies are now attempting to replicate the efficiency and coverage of groups such as the Sendero. They are encouraging informal networking and setting up intranet web sites where staff can post details about themselves and their work that they believe others might find interesting and useful. Other companies are formalizing the process by creating internal knowledge markets in which information is actually traded between business units.

There is little point, however, in moving information around the system if nobody knows what to do with it. Ultimately the job of sifting must be province of the intelligence analysts. To do the job properly they must also be extremely careful not to discourage staff from proffering information. If you reject the offer of information from a source it is unlikely the source will bother next time. The organizational culture must encourage a willingness to share information. All information generated from interpersonal interaction – be it words, moods or body language – is just the kind of subjective, informal information that the corporate memory must have to keep it alive and responsive.

Not only can this information be internally gathered, but it can also be fed back to the organization from meetings and observations of staff who travel and meet collaborators and competitors outside the organization. They can pass their findings back to an information management centre. Xerox, for instance, created what they call their 'national competitive database'. Sales and service reps are encouraged to use a 'competitive hot-line' to feed information as quickly as possible to the database. In that way analysts can be working on the material within 24 hours. In conjunction with the continual public opinion surveys and polls, the findings of the analytical staff form the basis of the benchmarking that Xerox see as a major tool in the company's strategic planning. Chevron runs a similar operation, which it calls its 'external technology watch' (ETW), as part of its benchmarking process. Whatever the name, it remains an intelligence-driven exercise.

Loyalty cards have become the electronic equivalent of coffee-shop gossip and they provide an increasingly important mechanism for gathering intelligence. Most mail order firms, for example, now have their own data management subsidiaries which, among other things, compile resident profiles, by postcode, permitting much tighter mail-shot targeting. Such companies used to flood an area and achieve only a 0.5 per cent return. Now, with much more accurate targeting, they are averaging over 30 per cent, sometimes hitting as high as 70 per cent. Boots's 'Advantage Card', for example, was able to target pregnant women and new mothers for mail order, reasoning that they would prefer to order for home delivery rather than walk. This micro-marketing, as it is called, enables sales information to be pinpointed and analyzed. From the analysis, strategy can be developed and implemented, and the results of the implementation tested – all in the time that previously would have been spent thinking about it.

there is no point gathering information if there are insufficient staff to analyze it

However, loyalty cards are increasingly being seen as an invasion of privacy. Companies are aware of this trend and are treading carefully – but they are still treading. The cards are also creating another problem producing a volume of information that is swamping the analysts – and there is no point gathering information if there are insufficient staff to analyze it. Analysis can be done either in-house or by out-sourcing the task to specialist intelligence firms. Employing your own staff is expensive, but cost-cutting in this area will be counter-productive. Outside firms can range from those who trawl the open source information to those who do whatever it takes to get whatever you want. There was an instance in 1998, for example, where *Punch* magazine staff were found rummaging around in the dustbins of NatWest and Coutts banks. The resultant articles were embarrassing for both banks.

Organizations must be prepared to defend themselves against offensive intelligence activities in both the elctronic intelligence (ELINT) and human intelligence (HUMINT) fields. In the commercial world ELINT can be equated most straightforwardly to computer crime, which itself can be split into three distinct categories:

- computer misuse
- computer-related crime
- computer-aided crime.

Computer misuse includes hacking, virus injection and malicious programming. It is a fact that the vast majority of firms have no intelligence or security structures in place to detect such misuse, let alone prevent it. Computer-related crime includes pornography, software copyright, information blackmail and spoofing. Computer-aided crime includes fraud, scanning forgery, telecom crime and theft. This list does not even begin to cover what the military are referring to as cyber-munitions, which will be the ammunition of the cyberwars of the future.

On the HUMINT side there are equivalents today of all five types of spies identified by Sun Tzu 2000 years ago:

- The *local* spy. Hired from the people of the locality – in business terms these are the knowledge workers headhunted from organizations who are in a position to have access to information on competitors or collaborators in the same market sector.

- The *inside* spy. Hired from enemy employees – someone who is on your pay-roll but remains inside a competitor's organization.

- The *reverse* spy. The inside spy of a competitor within your organization who has been turned by your intelligence – often referred to as double-agents.

- The *dead* spy. Someone working for you who has been identified by a competitor and is, therefore, of no further use to your organization.

- The *living* spy. Your own spy who survives and continues to operate.

Skilful use of assets means that everything is obtainable if you are prepared to commit the resources – if information exists then it is also gettable. The role of intelligence specialists is to identify the optimal method of collection and then to reconcile that with the resources at their disposal.

barriers

Putting procedures in place does not guarantee success. There will always be problems. Whilst it is the analyst (the human input) that gives competitive advantage in the intelligence process, at the same time it is human fallibility that is the biggest problem in the process. For example, a change of culture is often necessary to orient the intelligence function. This is especially difficult in the British business environment. The natural British obsession with secrecy, coupled with the culture of competition that is prevalent in the business community, means that organizations find it difficult to encourage inter-organizational competition while simultaneously discouraging intra-organizational competition. The culture of departmentalism, or 'silo'-ism, is endemic in British life and militates against the sharing of information that is essential for a dynamic intelligence function.

This is a problem not only at the organizational level, but also at the individual level. There are considerable difficulties in getting people to share knowledge that they consider would advance their own careers. As a consequence many individuals feel an understandable antipathy towards their intelligence departments. This antipathy, in turn, guarantees that the status of those departments remains low. As an example, many executives do not use the departments of their own firms but

human beings are simultaneously the intelligence function's greatest asset and its greatest liability

will instead turn to outside specialists. There are generally three reasons for this practice. First, they do not value their own colleagues; second, they do not wish their own colleagues to know what they are up to; third, they want the information they acquire to remain their own property. Human beings are, therefore, simultaneously the intelligence function's greatest asset and its greatest liability.

However, despite the importance of the human factor, we must not neglect the ever-increasing role played by technology in the intelligence process. The vast array of data-mining software now available has made the analyst's job immeasurably quicker. Statistical tools such as SPSS enhance data access, cleaning and selection; business query tools such as SQL allow on-line analytical processing or design sets; data visualization tools such as NETMAP graphically represent data in a manner that allows the identification of trends to become merely a pictorial task; and reporting software simplifies report creation. The purpose of these tools is to make the differentiation of signals and noise a relatively straightforward task. However, the sensible analyst will be wary of being driven solely by technology. Patterns and trends are no more than that – they are not proof. That is why the term 'data mining' is so appropriate. There are very few nuggets, but there is a great deal of fools' gold around – it needs an experienced miner to know the difference. There are also other problems with the technology. Results are only as good as the data entered – errors in entry will lead to erroneous results. Projects can be lengthy and expensive and results may be difficult to act upon. All of which returns us to the significance of the intelligence specialists. Their job is to tell the miners the most likely sites in which to dig, what to look for when they get there, and who to bring the results to when they find them.

To make organizations learning mechanisms they need a culture of 'dynamic inquisitiveness'. By this we mean organizations in which its members want to learn, want to know more, and are never satisfied with the current level, either personal or corporate, of knowledge at their disposal. Such organizations do not need to use the term competitive intelligence, they will, by their nature, be competitive organizations. The pay-off is that organizations with such a dynamic knowledge base will survive and prosper.

The analyst/expert is central to the development of an organization's intelligence, the growth of its knowledge base and, as a consequence, its competitive strategy. The acceptance of such a central role will require a change in culture – to one that encourages the sharing of information. It also requires an intelligence-friendly philosophy during the induction process so that new arrivals are imbued with an atmosphere of community. Above all, it must be understood that intelligence is both a *process* and a *product*. It is the analytical process that enables the transformation of disparate information into actionable strategic knowledge about the capabilities, intentions, performance and positioning of elements within the targeted environment. Simultaneously, intelligence is also the product of that process and it has to be appropriately packaged for the consumer – the decision maker. If organizations ignore this reality they are asking their business players to play blind – a course of action no CEO would seriously advocate. Whether knowledge is captured by capturing people or information, its significance as a major contributor to the competitive advantage of an organization is undeniable.

security

If an organization can successfully capture knowledge, how does it ensure it can keep it? This section looks at the security issues that have become prevalent in the electronic age. Best practice in security can simply be defined as keeping secure that which it is in the organization's interests to keep secure. The biggest problem for the security function is identifying what is actually valuable to the organization, rather than what is deemed valuable by management. Invariably management deems everything to be valuable. As a result, because it is not possible to secure everything, the attempt to do so means nothing is completely secure. An organization must choose between having a large percentage of its assets made partially secure or a small percentage of its assets made completely secure. Taking the latter approach has the added value of forcing the organization continually to monitor its assets. A consequence of continual monitoring is the diminishing likelihood that standard operating procedures will become routinized. The American phrase 'routinization corrodes sensitivity' should be the watch-phrase of every security organization. British troops in Northern Ireland very quickly learned that routine kills. The consequences are not so drastic in business, but the principle remains the same.

The basic principles of security can be applied to all aspects of the business game. The easiest way to access knowledge is to acquire the person with the knowledge. Physical security of personnel should not, therefore, be neglected because of the concentration on electronic security. The problem for organizations is to establish to what extent surveillance of their own, and others', employees is either legal or ethical. How can organizations protect these valuable human assets without gathering knowledge about them? The snooping capabilities available to and used by companies is alarming. Such bugging, 'grassing' and 'whistle-blowing' are not only intrusive but can also be counter-productive. Employees *will* become aware of covert surveillance – it is only a matter of time. When they do, they will be effectively lost to the organization. Any level of loyalty will be eradicated by the lack of trust indicated by bugging. In a culture of knowledge-sharing transparency, which we advocate throughout this book, such methods of internal surveillance would be inappropriate and unnecessary. We advocate transparency and sharing not for ethical but for efficiency reasons.

the resources needed to spy on employees are rarely worth the effort and the distrust engendered is a destructive force

The resources needed to spy on employees are rarely worth the effort and the distrust engendered is a destructive force.

The main concern for most organizations is e-security. In an age made chaotic by the anarchic structure of the Internet, how do organizations protect themselves from hackers, viruses, and cyber-terrorism? First they must define what is valuable. The good news is that those responsible for cyber-security have recognized that complete security is not possible. As a consequence, organizations are establishing integrated security strategies that accept the imperfections of electronic systems and make contingency plans that include legal and insurance support in the event of security breaches. British insurance companies are creating what are being called cyber-liability policies. These policies cover breaches of rights (confidentiality issues), hacking, cyber-vandalism and fraud.

According to the security consultancy, Information Risk Management, more than half of the largest UK companies do not have any formal e-security policies in place. Currently there are an estimated 50000 computer bugs with 500 plus new bugs arriving every month. Most companies are either ignorant of the problem or unwilling to do much about it. High-profile breaches such as the Melissa virus, which affected Microsoft's Hotmail service, as well as Intel and Lucent systems, are only a tiny proportion of the breaches that occur. Research by Information Risk Management indicates that over 70 per cent of Fortune 1000 companies have privately admitted they had been targeted by information spies. A DTI survey puts the figure at 90 per cent. What is just as worrying is that 88 per cent had not reported the attacks to the police. These include the attacks from within the company, which can account for as much as 40 per cent of malicious interventions. It is a Catch 22 situation. Report the break-in and you look vulnerable; don't report it and you *are* vulnerable. Unfortunately, looking vulnerable creates a loss of confidence and a consequent drop in share value. The infamous 1994 attacker at Citibank is reported to have transferred $10 million out of the bank. The related loss of confidence and business was estimated to be in billions. The truth is that all organizations are vulnerable – it is only the degree that is in question.

'Backdoor' or 'Trojan Horse' programs can be injected into the desktop computers of targeted individuals so that at a later date the hackers can gain easy entry to those computers. These Trojan Horse programs, such as Back Office 2000, are the work of cyber-vandals like the Cult of the Dead Cow, a group of self-confessed cyber-missionaries, or hackers to the rest of us. These groups actually hold their own conventions, which are attended not only by other like-minded groups but also by computer security professionals, law enforcement agencies and intelligence analysts and officials. Whatever the motivation of such groups, they pose a considerable threat to the e-security of the corporate world. Ironically, they also act as unpaid security-system testers. The nature of security is that there will always exist an escalatory process of attack and defence. Organizations can only attempt to stay ahead of the game by establishing a formal security policy that:

● identifies the reason why security is needed (security for its own sake is counter-productive);

● appreciates what levels of security are appropriate and where and to whom they should be applied;

- trains well;
- implements measures to recover after a breach;
- constantly reviews policy;
- modifies policy in light of review findings;
- encourages a culture of vigilant appraisal of all aspects of the security function.

To minimize e-security breaches, your company should also:

- regularly review its policies – installing a firewall is no protection on its own;
- never forget the human factor – educate your people in such practices as password management and breach reporting procedures;
- ensure the security of your back-up systems as well as primary systems;
- have a procedure for sensing changes to the system;
- have a procedure to identify those with authority to change the system;
- identify who manages security;
- identify who determines access privileges.

The most important aspect of a security policy is to develop it in relation to the needs of the game. Policies should be based on the answer to one simple question – what will information security add to our chances of success in the game? If the answer is nothing, then don't secure it. Only secure those assets that add value to the organization. Too much information is kept secret because its guardians are not sure of its significance. The expert player knows what is important.

only secure those assets that add value to the organization

knowledge management

Once we have acquired knowledge (intelligence) and retained it (security), how precisely do we manage it? Knowledge management is the term that has been used to describe the new business environment that has emerged from the flatter organizational structures of the late 1980s and early 1990s, replacing 'received wisdom', 'corporate memory' and 'corporate knowledge'. The ability of organizations to be able to access the new volume of information meant that they began to reinvent themselves. The once fashionable notion of business process re-engineering (BPR) was built on the new information technologies. The technologies enabled horizontal, team-based processes to supercede the old departmentally oriented 'silos' of the past. Bill Gates's digital nervous system is merely a logical extension of BPR. Having reconstructed themselves, organizations were then in a position to take advantage of the environmental change that the Internet generated.

One of the ways they did this was to 'converge' previously distinct domains. For example, we can see, on a daily basis, the convergence of the telecoms, computing and service provider domains. As a consequence, a link between AT&T, Microsoft and Disney makes perfect sense. This is only the beginning because the information convergence will inevitably become deeper. The smart business player is already planning how to take advantage of such convergence. However, in order for organizations to take advantage of the opportunities out there they need staff with the requisite skills. Hence the 'knowledge worker' syndrome. Companies need workers with high skill levels and high flexibility. It has been estimated that up to 80 per cent of all jobs in the USA are 'cerebral' (Wykoff, 1996). Organizations are now enmeshed in this accelerating change and must respond or die. Technology allows information to be available almost instantaneously and as a consequence decisions will be needed more speedily and companies will be looking for staff who can deliver on cerebral tasks. This means that the manner in which organizations manage their knowledge will have to change radically.

For staff to learn continuously there must be a culture of learning. The notion that a culture of learning was crucial to organizational success was first articulated in the late 1980s when Hayes *et al.* in the USA (1988) and Pedler *et al.* in the UK (1997) first wrote about learning organizations. From there we had, among others, Nonaka and Takeuchi talking about the knowledge-creating company (1995) and Peter Senge (1994), who looked at the practices necessary to extract competitive advantage from a learning organization. What all analysts of learning organizations agreed upon were the common threads that characterized such organizations. These are:

- the pace of change in the environment, which a company has to replicate in its own environment;
- staff-centric approaches such as self-development, employee participation and increased delegation;
- a major reorientation of systems and structures of management;
- a redistribution of power and control in which the old, hierarchical models, where those at the top dispense knowledge in the form of pre-packaged solutions, are transformed into societies where co-operation, teamwork and mutual support dominate the learning process;
- a culture of transparency and sharing.

These five characteristics come down to a simple definition: 'a learning organization is one in which a culture of sharing knowledge is immediately apparent even to the most casual of external observers'.

Those who wish to share knowledge are those who truly value it. Those who wish to retain knowledge for themselves are those who have misunderstood its value. The greater the knowledge of the individual members of an organization about that organization and its environment, the greater can be their contribution to the organization. The greater the spread of that knowledge, the greater the chance that it can be preserved by the organization. The last point is particularly hard for organizations to accept because they feel that knowledge that belongs to the company must not be allowed to leave it, since it might be of advantage to competitors. This is to confuse information with knowledge. Part of the knowledge is the socialization that transformed the information into knowledge. That cannot be replicated – the *company* will retain that type of knowledge. Organizations must, therefore, actually encourage challenges to existing assumptions – what Nonaka calls the 'articulation' process: the conversion of tacit knowledge to explicit knowledge. However, such an approach is an anathema to most corporate business players who maintain that their personal contribution to the company, and consequently their rewards, will be judged by *their* sales figures, *their* performance indicators. In many, if not most cases, that assessment is correct.

those who wish to share knowledge are those who truly value it

In the true learning organization, however, it will not be the case. One of the great successes of this approach was made by the BP Amoco group after the merger of the two original companies. The new group developed a 'performance processes and learning team' with a somewhat missionary brief, 'to capture, share and utilize the vast quantities of knowledge throughout the company'. On a fundamental level it achieved a remarkable feat. It gained acceptance for the idea that the most basic learning process of stopping, reflecting, learning and moving on, was a value-added operation. Chris Collinson, one of BP Amoco's learning team, said that when they revisited business units 'to find out what effect [the approach] had on their business, we had no problem surpassing our target of $100 million of added value' (*Financial Times*, 28 April 1999). In rich learning organizations, performance is judged by the contribution an individual makes to the team. Stars will only remain stars if they contribute to the team.

One of the footballing success stories of the 1990s was Marcello Lippi's rejuvenation of Juventus. Over a four-year period Juve won three Italian League titles, appeared in three Champions League finals (winning one) and one UEFA Cup final. In that period Lippi changed the whole approach to personnel. Players were bought in their ascendancy, often from small clubs, and then sold after relatively

short periods. During their time at Juve their value increased and they were consequently sold at a profit. This meant that Juve was able to cut cost by buying players
on relatively low salaries and selling them on before their contracts expired and salaries would have had to be renegotiated. However, cost was only one reason for high turnover. The other was that it made playing sense. As Lippi himself said, 'There is only one way to motivate players every time, and that is to appeal to the things they have not yet achieved'. What Juve is effectively doing is bringing in knowledge workers (consultants) and releasing them when the job is done.

> here is only one way to motivate players every time, and that is to appeal to the things they have not yet achieved

What does such a policy do to the beloved team spirit? Lippi does not foster
team spirit or develop it, he imposes it. Everyone plays for the team because it is
in their own best interests. The message is that a championship winner is a more
valuable commodity to potential buyers. It is, therefore, in the individuals' interest
for the team to succeed. Team spirit is both a consequence of and a reason for
success. However, the reverse is also true. If success starts to wane, so too does team
spirit. Imported individuals may then have little residual loyalty to the organization.

What the good learning organization does is to integrate two models. Like
Ferguson's Manchester United, it creates team spirit by a youth (development)
policy through which groups of knowledge workers progress to the first team;
simultaneously it follows Lippi's Juventus and imports established stars from
whom the youngsters can learn good habits. Selection of those imported players,
therefore, becomes crucial. In that way corporate knowledge increases, because the
knowledge extracted is tacit knowledge that has previously been lost to organizations when personnel move on.

Extracting this knowledge in the relatively small confines of a football club is
easier than the same task in large multi-nationals with thousands of employees,
diversely located. This is where technology comes into its own. Electronic communication systems, mobile phones, video-conferencing and group-ware all make
sharing information easier, but it does not make it happen. That only occurs when
the culture to do so is in place. In other words, when the incentives to share are
greater than the incentives to hoard. How can this be achieved? By demonstrating
the values of freeing and sharing knowledge, and then by rewarding those who do
demonstrate that ability. Pilot projects, for example, can be used to illustrate the
benefits of knowledge sharing, but gaining acceptance even for limited pilots is
often very difficult. The very intangibility of the product (knowledge) that organizations try to sell to their people makes the sale difficult. However, like most good

products, once people have bought it they will wonder how they ever managed to get by without it.

using the knowledge

Having captured, protected and managed knowledge on behalf of the organization, how does the smart player use that knowledge for competitive advantage? The key to using knowledge is identifying the business objective to which the knowledge will be applied. Capturing and managing knowledge for its own sake will not add competitive advantage. Knowledge must be captured and managed for a reason. This avoids potentially damaging information overload. The Internet had more connections in its first ten years than the telephone in its first 50; the number of books in libraries is doubling every 10 years; nearly 10000 periodicals are released in the USA, every day; at least 1000 books are released daily worldwide; more information has been created in the last 30 years than the previous 5000 and it is doubling every 5 years; online databases are proliferating at a phenomenal rate; and the information flooding onto the Internet appears infinite. We are drowning in information and it will be the organizations that are most selective in its use that will have the competitive advantage.

knowledge must be captured and managed for a reason

The information flow can be controlled not only by expanding the capability to process the information, but also by contracting the volume of information to be processed. The most urgent problem for organizations to deal with is perhaps that of e-mail. At Sun Microsystems an insider reported that the average employee processes 120 messages per day. One manager commented, 'The urgent is driving out the important.' The Novell organization reports that at any one time 1.4 per cent of the workforce is dealing with 'spam' messages. As with all communications, there are simple rules that are transferable from more traditional media. Just as it is possible to discern from the packaging whether a letter is worth opening, the same is true of e-mail. Not everybody needs to see your communications, so be sparing when forwarding. Use the most appropriate medium – link use to the medium. If possible, establish strict, and enforceable, rules for e-mail usage, or at least establish guidelines that employees are requested to abide by. Create business environments that encourage personal contact and minimize the over-reliance on the electronic methods.

This advice deals with the impediments to the effective use of knowledge. What advice is there to enhance the use of knowledge? The answer is once again the correct use of the human analyst. When the volume of information is such that it is literally impossible to process, the professional analyst becomes even more vital. Even if trends and patterns have been identified by technological procedures such as data-mining, the analyst must still select which trends are significant in relation to the goals of the organization – that takes judgement. There are no rules as to exactly when knowledge should or should not be used for competitive advantage – hence the importance of the smart player. Knowledge is not power, it is merely latent power. Knowledge must be infused with the intuition that the game's players bring to it.

The most effective way to use the knowledge cycle is to apply it to the *motivation*, *others*, *rules*, *environment* and *skills* of the game (*see* Fig. 7.4). Success depends, therefore, on the players' knowledge of the game. Genuine knowledge management is not a fad, it's a necessity.

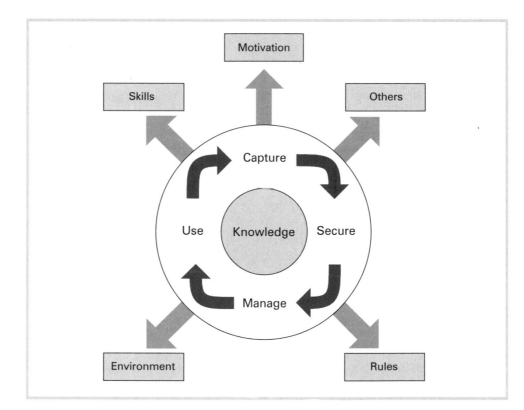

Figure 7.4 Applying the knowledge cycle

chapter 8

coaching

how can we teach what we know?

Coaching must not be confused with counselling or mentoring which are concerned with the well-being of the individual. Coaching is concerned with the well-being of the individual and group only in as much as it affects performance. Coaches must never lose sight of the centrality of performance.

Success does not simply happen, it is the result of hard work. It is the application and implementation of players' knowledge of the game being played. The player has yet to be born who has achieved their potential on their own. All players need *coaching*. This chapter identifies best practices in coaching and suggest ways of developing and maintaining such practices. However, using the term 'coaching' in a business context has a major disadvantage because the analogy is too readily associated with sport. In sport, the individuals or teams being coached essentially all want to be where they are. They would probably play for nothing. Many of the coaching problems in business involve players who would rather be elsewhere. The awful morale problems experienced in call-centre businesses are a classic example. But the analogy is still highly relevant. This is because at its core all coaching – in business, war, sport or entertainment – is performance related.

what is coaching?

Coaching is the ability of an individual (the coach) to release the potential of the coachee(s) in order to raise the coachee's performance to the maximum level possible. It is the centrality of performance that differentiates coaching from mentoring or counselling. Coaches are not concerned with the individual per se, they are only concerned with performance. This philosophy applies equally to teams, groups and individuals. Clearly there are different practical considerations in coaching one-to-one with a tennis player or with a CEO than with coaching a football team or an entire workforce. However, the underlying principles remain the same. The coaching cycle shown in Fig. 8.1 should be applied to every coaching situation. This cycle is equally as applicable to the individual, the work group, the team, the company or the organization.

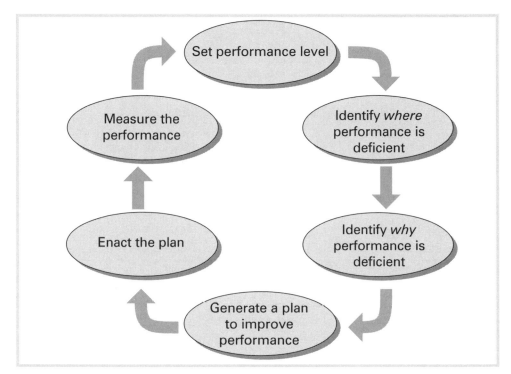

Figure 8.1 The coaching cycle

The terms *set, identify, generate, enact,* and *measure* are carefully chosen:

● Setting the desired performance level is essential to the overall success of the coaching process. Without some notion of what excellent performance looks like there is little chance that any coaching intervention will be useful. This does not mean merely benchmarking against others. If you are pre-eminent in your field, set your own targets. However, they must be realistic – unrealistically high targets are counter-productive.

● To identify deficiencies involves a process of observation, which is central to the coaching process. It is pointless for a coach to enter an environment and take at face value the complaints and analyses of the current staff. An incoming coach must have an observation period in order that the identification of performance deficiencies is as unbiased as possible.

- The coaching plan must be generated by the interaction between the coach and players.

- The plan can be enacted only after both groups have agreed on its structure.

- Performance can then be measured against the agreed structure and any deficiencies identified such that the cycle can be repeated.

Just as the coaching process is never-ending in a temporal sense, so too is it never-ending in a hierarchical sense. Throughout any organization individuals will simultaneously be both coaches and players. Imagine a CEO, for example.

throughout any organization individuals will simultaneously be both coaches and players

CEOs should be the coaches of their executive teams, but simultaneously they must be players against other CEOs and within their own boards. They will need coaching themselves in order to improve their own performances. So it cascades down the organization. Everyone will, at some stage, be involved in both playing (carrying out operational tasks) or coaching (enabling someone else to carry out operational tasks more effectively).

The most neglected aspect of coaching, and also the most difficult, is coaching the coaches. If the CEO is expected to coach the executive team, then who coaches the CEO? Increasingly it is a task being handed to outside agencies. However, because there is insufficient understanding about accurate performance criteria, such outsourcing is at best irrelevant and at worst counter-productive. If the CEOs, managers or supervisors do not understand that their primary task is the improvement of the performance of those who report directly to them, then they cannot themselves be coached. Performance when coaching coaches can only be measured against pre-determined and well constructed criteria. We act as coaching advisers to Cape Consulting, a service excellence consultancy, which has run a pilot coaching scheme with Virgin Atlantic. The most difficult task facing Virgin was how to measure the effectiveness of our intervention. We might, for example, claim that we had improved the coaching skills of their management staff, and the staff may even agree, but how could Virgin measure our claims and prove that our intervention provided added value? What was needed was a major reassessment of the performance criteria that Virgin Atlantic demanded from their players. Virgin have, consequently, embarked on a major overhaul of their service philosophy. Called 'coaching for service excellence' it entails developing a working culture that has performance at its heart.

Coaching interventions must also be continual. The coach should anticipate unacceptable key performance indicator (KPI) figures and intervene; and the coach should recognize if the KPIs are being too easily achieved and raise the service level agreement (SLA). The coach should continually monitor performance and attempt to improve it. The effectiveness of such a coaching-oriented approach answers the often-asked question, 'What is the role of a manager?' The first principle of good management is to make yourself redundant, in an operational sense. Mountains of research indicate that managers feel they spend too much time on their day-to-day job and have insufficient time to devote to strategic planning, surveying the environment, sifting alternatives and measuring the competition. But if they think that then they have misunderstood what their job is. They must understand that their job is to improve and maintain the performance of their players – otherwise they are in the wrong job.

The problem is that a majority of managers *are* in the wrong job. They may have been the best, or the longest serving player, but that does not make them ideal managers. Staff development *is* the manager's job because competent coaches (managers) improve the performance of their players by utilizing the learning opportunities present in operational activity, in a planned and guided manner. If managers fulfil that single, crucial role they will add more value to the organization than by any amount of operational tinkering.

who delivers?

If coaching adds so much value, how is it done? How is good coaching delivered to, or by, an organization? To be truly effective three elements of the delivery process must be isolated and given due consideration. These elements are *who* delivers it, what *practices* are at their disposal and what *vehicles* are available for the delivery.

The 'who' question is extremely important and often ignored. The argument usually runs that anyone in an organization can coach. However, it is also true that anyone can play, but you would still choose Tiger Woods on your team rather than virtually anybody else. Similarly with coaches, some people are just better at it than others. It is vital that those who have the qualities and skills to coach should be encouraged to do so. The encouragement should be reinforced by a reward system that recognizes the added value the coaching provides for the organization. If the old adage that an organization's most valued assets are its staff, then it is bizarre that those charged with the development and performance of those assets are themselves undervalued. It is especially strange in knowledge organizations where the coaches are, in effect, the product developers.

However, getting the right people is a problem since coaching is often seen as representing value for the staff but not the organization. Directors are coached to relieve stress, managers are coached to manage time, staff are coached to make them happier. While all of the above may be important they are only important if they positively affect performance. Great coaches understand their players so well that they know what is the appropriate intervention for each individual within the constraints of the group. What is it that distinguishes Ferguson from Venables or Hoddle or Howard Wilkinson or Annie Jacquet or Arsene Wenger? They are all coaches, but they all have their own individual styles and those individual styles will also be, in part, linked to other factors such as gender and nationality. The UK has seen, for example, the emergence of foreign coaches such as Wenger (Arsenal), Houllier (Liverpool) and Vialli (Chelsea). Has their success been because of, or in spite of, their nationality? The answer is a complicated mixture of individual and national characteristics. Different countries do have different styles of management and coaching.

> great coaches understand their players so well that they know what is the appropriate intervention for each individual within the constraints of the group

These differences are also recognized across the business spectrum. Bosch, the German industrial group, for example, has established a joint project with Pittsburg's Carnegie-Mellon University in order to train upwards of 40 German staff a year in American management techniques. According to the president of the new Carnegie-Bosch Institute, the 'US management style is sufficiently different from the European one. The Germans in particular seem to benefit from coming here and learning something valuable' (*Financial Times*, 22 July 1999). In Eastern Europe there is still a marked reluctance to invest in training programmes, which means that coaching remains a low status activity and a barrier to economic expansion. Interestingly, if the former Soviet-bloc countries were to take a leaf from the coaching books of their sports academies they might be more successful. The meticulous planning of their sports coaches is legendary. They manage to liberate their players within the boundaries of rigid team discipline. Flair, creativity and individuality are allowed, providing they contribute to the achievement of the team's goals. It is a principle that should be the bedrock of all organizational behaviour. So it is clearly worthwhile searching abroad for coaching talent that provide added value to your organization. However, never choose a coach just because of nationality and never reject them just because of nationality. The same principle should apply to gender. Whoever you choose – whether male or female – should exhibit the qualities of excellent coaches.

Typically, excellent coaches are able to:

● be consistent – because staff do not forgive inconsistency easily; also if players cannot be sure of the validity of instructions from one minute to the next they will tend to delay before acting upon them;

● be positive – it encourages high expectations;

● share knowledge – it aids delegation which creates time;

● establish trust – it develops staff confidence in you;

● intelligently observe – it provides the knowledge;

● question sensitively – another aspect of knowledge gathering;

● listen attentively – more knowledge gathering;

● help coaches to understand how they learn best – everyone learns in different ways;

● provide tailored feedback – it should be relevant and thoughtful.

When we ask who delivers coaching, the answer is simple: the person who exhibits most of the qualities and skills described above. Think of a good coach from your own experience and now match your role model to this skill set: you will find an exact fit.

Coaches are not there to alter people, they are there to alter performance. Advice must, therefore, be situational not abstract. It must be concerned with real events in the working life of the coachee. White-water rafting does not prepare for the workplace, it prepares for white-water rafting. In an article in the *Financial Times* (7 December 1999) Robert Ford, Microsoft's' director of IT for Europe, Middle East and Africa, said of a particularly strenuous activity with the Royal Navy: 'I wanted to put them under tremendous amounts of pressure', because 'people develop personal skills by being pushed to do things they would not normally choose'. What he is describing is not coaching. Coaches should seek to generate the urgency and development of personal skills within scenarios familiar to the coachees. The mantra of the good coach must be 'make it real'. It is difficult to understand what people who spend their working lives tapping computer keyboards and talking on the telephone have to gain from knowing how to stop a ship sinking.

coaches are not there to alter people, they are there to alter performance

Feedback must be based on specific observation, not on inferences made by the coach. The coachee must be able to recall the events that have been observed, so that a connection can be established between coach and coachee. The same principal demands that the coach should be descriptive and not judgmental in the delivery of feedback, since the latter can damage the coaching relationship and inject negativity into the situation. It is also important for the coach to provide a series of alternative routes for the coachee to embark upon, rather than simply to suggest solutions. In that way coachees will come to their own solution and be more committed to it. Coaches must also remember that the provision of feedback should be must be coachee-centric. It must be delivered when the coachee can take it, in the form and quantities most appropriate for the coachee. The coach must also distinguish when the feedback needs to be motivational rather than informational – so acknowledging the needs of the coachee and giving those needs a central place in any activities.

The final element of the 'who' of coaching concerns personal style. Every individual has their own style; what coaches must do is identify their own style, identify other styles and identify the style most appropriate to the situation. It then becomes the coach's task either to adjust their own style or to get a colleague with a more appropriate style to assist. Coaching styles exist on a continuum, with 'directing' at one extreme and 'facilitating' at the other (*see* Fig. 8.2). These styles are all concerned with performance, as is also the selection of an appropriate style (*see* Fig 8.3).

	Directing ◄──────────────► Facilitating	
Style	Confronting, prescribing, informing	Catalytic, cathartic, supporting
Description	Telling, providing detailed recommendations, imparting information, directing the coachee in specific tasks	Encouraging, exploring issues in open discussion, supporting where confidence is low

Figure 8.2 Coaching styles

Selection guide

Directing ◄──────────────► Facilitating

- Underperformers
- Those who ask for direction
- When coachee has poor self-insight
- When coachee is unclear what constitutes success
- When there is immediate risk to operations

- High performers, self-motivated
- Those who ask for encouragement
- When coachee has good self-insight
- Where the criteria for success are clearly understood
- When there is long-term risk to operations

Figure 8.3 Selecting an appropriate coaching style

vehicles of delivery

If we now know who the coach should be we can also begin to answer questions concerning the vehicles of delivery. It must be emphasized, however, that the vehicle will always be subordinate to the coach. Good coaches can deliver coaching sat one-to-one at a coffee table with no delivery vehicle other than themselves. However, the good coach will also be very precise about delivery vehicles. The mechanism used for learning clearly has an important bearing on the quality of the learning experience and a happy marriage between coach and vehicle always adds value to the coaching process. Our concept of delivery includes business schools at one end of the scale and simple board games at the other end. The coaching of business players may occur during an MBA, within their own organizations, at corporate universities or from outside coaching consultants. Some would argue that MBA courses should not be concerned with coaching. Look again at Fig. 8.3 and the criteria at the facilitative end of the continuum – they virtually describe the modern MBA student.

Over-reliance on a single educative style is a dangerous practice. Harvard's preoccupation with case teaching turns out graduates who are expert in dealing with cases but not necessarily with reality. Cases, however well designed, are essentially abstract and as such have no greater validity then any other seminar-based educational process. The dominance of case teaching is the result of laziness and insufficient educational analysis prior to the selection of delivery methods. Anyone who saw the 1999 TV series *Masters of Universe*, which dealt with the McKinsey consultancy's methods, saw, in one exercise, the complete ignorance of the 'people' factor by most of the staff – with a few honourable exceptions. Case teaching cannot prepare (coach) you for realistic management difficulties.

coaching 'events' not connected to real situations are of limited value

Similarly, coaching 'events' not connected to real situations are of limited value. Why, for example, do business organizations pay good money for the privilege of hearing Gulf-War veteran John Nichol recount his experience as a captive of the Iraqis? To be fair to Nichol, he is as bemused as we are about his success on the business speaking circuit (*Financial Times*, 11 December 1999). Good coaching must be based upon a clearly defined understanding of the learning process – an understanding that seems to be in short supply.

What role should the coach play as delivery vehicles become more sophisticated? This is probably the most important dilemma the modern coach faces. Business simulation games are becoming more and more realistic. Board game simulations such as the Manufacturing Game (http://www.mfg-game.com), the

Beer Game, Tango (www.celemi.com) and many others have been a staple ingredient of management training diets for over 30 years. However, the arrival on the business scene of the 'Nintendo children' – people born post-1970 and raised on computer games – will demand a new approach to business education. For the under-30s playing computer games and working are indistinguishable. Computer and video games have inbuilt complexity of the type that abounds in modern business. Game playing is not simply preparation for work. Achievement in games is the dominant ethic.

The new generation is already affecting the way work gets done. Financial companies are inventing game-like trading interfaces in which winning the game means making an actual profit. New associates at Bankers Trust, for example, learn about the bank's policies by playing a customer-focused video game. The gaming preference is also influencing the workplace in the move towards less formality. The coaching message is clear – deliver via a relevant, contemporary vehicle or risk losing your coachees.

The drift towards this merging of business simulations with computer games is inexorable and is termed 'edutainment'. The problem is that, as with case studies, no real research has been done to validate the added educational value that such methods provide. Langley and Larsen (1995) suggest that the game alone is not an appropriate learning tool, and a structured learning environment in which to embed the game is necessary. While such an arrangement may be useful and complement the learning value of games, we can find no irrefutable evidence that it is necessary. We have collaborated with a successful commercial games designer who argues even more forcefully than we do that game playing of itself develops all the generic skills required to play the business game successfully.

Demis Hassabis, the 22-year-old Managing Director of Elixir-Studios, believes that expertise in just three games does generate the complete skill base for the business game. Those three games are poker, chess and diplomacy. Mastering those games, he claims, will engage all the necessary skills. We agree that simply playing those games, or other more technologically sophisticated edutainment games, does develop an understanding of the links between structure and behaviour. And that is precisely the coaching dilemma. If game playing can do this, where does the coach come in? The coach becomes a pure facilitator or enabler. The coach only intervenes when success in the game playing has been eluding the player, or when the player seeks advice. The other crucial role the coach plays is in the selection of the games to be played.

However, most business players are not prepared to make the intellectual leap necessary to extract full advantage from Hassabis's mixture of poker, chess and diplomacy. They have an emotional need to locate the games in a quasi-business 'reality'. This is why companies such as MBAgames.com are busy marketing their web-based game Conglomerate, which enables players to take part from anywhere in the world. While not yet able to learn (i.e. be artificially intelligent) such games are still an advance on simulations such as SimCity. In our collaboration with Elixir-Studios we are seeking to develop virtual business environments similar to the entire country they have modelled in their latest game, Revolution. This is the next step towards a virtual business world in which players can immerse themselves in any aspect of the business game.

The coach's role would then also be replicated in the game. Coaches would be able to manipulate the game in order to develop experiential learning as they deemed necessary. Coaches will not become any more or less important: their job will still be to improve performance. What virtual game playing will provide is a mechanism for speeding up experiential learning at less cost, in terms of real mistakes, to the organization. In the

business coaches must begin to explore the learning potential of computer strategy games

meantime business coaches must begin to explore the learning potential of computer strategy games already available and mix and match with other media in order to provide the type of multimedia experience that the under-30s expect and demand. Why not, for example, use Championship Manager 2000, the football management game, in conjunction with Deloitte Touche's annual premiership business analysis? Or possibly combine the insights gained from *Saving Private Ryan* with those derived from playing Tiberian Sun, the command and control strategy game? Any of these options are open to the imaginative coach – as long as they link with the real. Do not forget, however, that if it does not improve performance, it is bad coaching.

practices

'Practices' refer to the ways in which coaches go about their jobs – they are the essential building blocks of any coaching relationship. A distinction must be made between the internal coach and the external consultant. The advantages of consultants are well known: they provide a 'new' perspective, they can be relatively objective and they carry less baggage than those already in the organization. However, they also have no commitment to the organization, their relationship with their coachees is transitory and they can be viewed with suspicion by those within the organization. The model we use when acting as external coaching consultants is to build slowly to the point where we can enter the coaching cycle. The stages of the model, shown in Fig. 8.4, are:

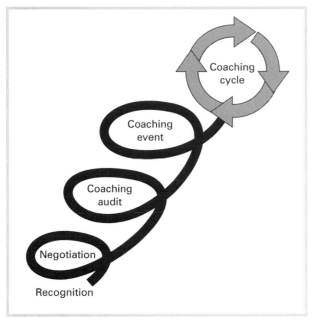

Figure 8.4 The steps towards the coaching cycle

- *Recognition* by the host organization that there is some value to be derived from coaching. This can occur as the result of either pain (the company is in trouble), fear (the company anticipates trouble) or strategy (the company wishes to avoid trouble).

- *Negotiation* – we agree with the organization the process of implementation and internal marketing of the coaching programme.

- *Coaching audit* – between three and five days of intense observation of the environment and working practices of the coachees. This enables us to build up the confidence of the coachees so that they do not view us as a threat.

- *Coaching event* – usually a one-day workshop that demonstrates the value of coaching practices to both the individual and the organization. It is at this stage that the coachees should accept the programme – if they are not convinced then we have failed to do our job.

On completion of the final stage we develop, in conjunction with the coachees, individual coaching programmes based on the elements of the coaching cycle. Once in the coaching cycle, the best practices of coaching are the same for internal or external coaches.

One of the most important, and neglected, aspects of coaching is planning. This is not the simple mechanics of timetabling or organizing the tools and logistics, but the detailed thinking about the strategic, tactical and operational requirements of a project of any length. For any project the principles are identical:

- identify objectives
- develop strategy
- determine resources: what is necessary and what is available
- decide how you will apply those resources
- decide how you will evaluate the product.

It is this planning process that the coach must follow in order to succeed.

At the crucial moment in England's 1998 World Cup campaign a lack of planning cost them dearly. Their coach, Glen Hoddle, failed to plan for the possibility of a penalty shoot-out and ended up in a situation where David Batty, who had never taken a penalty at senior-level football, was given the task of taking a vital penalty. Hoddle said that you could not practise penalties because the pressures of reality are different. True, but why then does Tiger Woods practise thousands of putts every day? Because skill is technique under pressure. The stronger the technique, the more pressure it can withstand. Confidence in technique is developed through practice.

confidence in technique is developed through practice

Hoddle's ineptitude demonstrates another vital aspect of coaching practice: when and how to take responsibility. Accepting responsibility has two benefits. First, it relieves pressure from the coachee. If the coach selects you for a task, rather than you volunteering, it indicates confidence in your ability. Second, it demonstrates a willingness by the coach to accept equality of commitment to the team. Hoddle always appears reluctant to accept blame. If things went badly, it was divine retribution. Teams will not stay loyal to a coach they perceive as unwilling to accept a fair share of the responsibility.

Performance excellence relies also on the mindsets of the players. In the mid-1970s Tim Gallwey of Harvard wrote the first book in what has become a series. It was called *The Inner Game of Tennis* and dealt with the mental aspects of game playing. The latest in the series is *The Inner Game of Work* (1999). Gallwey claims that the most difficult opponent to confront is 'the opponent within one's own head'. Business coaches who do not demand excellence are failing their coachees. But no matter how demanding the coach, if the coachee lacks the mental approach to succeed, then the coach will be relatively ineffective. There is an old maxim in sport that transfers precisely to business: 'Everyone has the will to win, only the excellent have the will to prepare to win.'

Good coaches can get their players into the right zone but they cannot do the job for them; ultimately the players must play the game. The coach must be able to distinguish between performance and style. It is not enough to look good, you must produce a performance. In business too it is easy to be seduced by style. It is the coach's job to do whatever it takes to foster the will to win and also to stay successful. This is achieved by the selection of appropriate coaching activities and with careful planning. Coaching activities must be designed to be 'real' for each coachee. Factors which affect the selection of coaching activities are shown in Fig. 8.5.

The selection of the coaching activity will depend on which factor is considered most significant to performance enhancement. As a consequence, the coaching delivery process can be represented as in Fig. 8.6. Throughout the process, virtually

Factor		Coaching activities
Situational	$\Longrightarrow$	Reframing, rehearsing, testing new behaviours
Motivational	$\Longrightarrow$	Goal setting, confidence building, learning to learn
Skills	$\Longrightarrow$	Modelling, practice, training, realistic targeting
Experience	$\Longrightarrow$	Role enlargement, delegation, environmental awareness, training
Temperament	$\Longrightarrow$	Promoting self-insight, feedback, external coaching and counselling

Figure 8.5 Selecting appropriate coaching activities

every aspect will come into play at some stage as the coaching spotlight is turned on each one of the MORES (*see* Fig. 8.7).

This process then provides straightforward answers to the basic questions of coaching:

● What is coaching? It is the art of raising and maintaining performance.

● When should coaching occur? Continually.

● Why should we coach? Because performance cannot improve without it.

● How can we measure the performance of the coach? By measuring the performance of the coachees.

Coaching is not just for the workers – it is for everyone in the organization. It is a way of doing business that adds value. It adds value because it liberates. Good coaches take the performance of their coachees beyond the limits of the coach's own knowledge, so that both coach and coachee are learning in an iterative relationship. Good coaching facilitates learning – and the business world is striving for learning organizations.

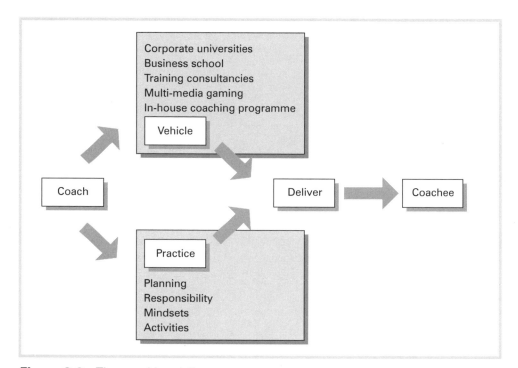

Figure 8.6 The coaching delivery process

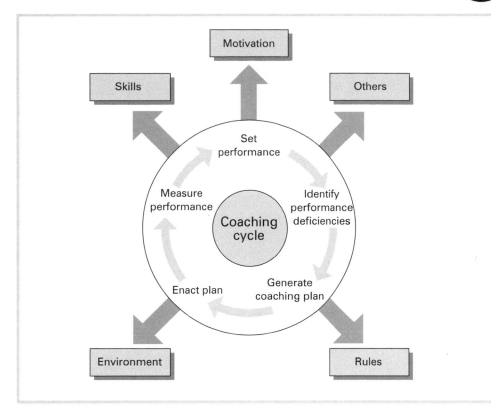

Figure 8.7 Linking the coaching cycle with the MORES

exploiting

how can we use what we know?

The effective management of knowledge and coaching of people enables opportunities to be identified – the best players seize those opportunities and exploit them.

It is now up to you, the reader, to transform the information from the previous chapters into knowledge. Ultimately you will test that knowledge against your own future experiences and convert it to wisdom. In this chapter we will share with you our knowledge about game playing as we have developed it. It is your job to test it against *your* reality – it may or may not be right for you. There are just four simple stages in playing any game successfully (*see* Fig. 9.1) but the work required to implement them is enormous.

identifying the game

What type of game are you about to play, or are already playing? Is it competitive, co-operative or co-opetive? Is it the right game for you? What other games are being played simultaneously? How do you prioritize which games to play and when? The answers to such questions are central to success. Game players often fail because of their inability to identify accurately the game in which they are engaged. The first task is to ascertain what game the others in your business are playing. Are they playing the same game as you, or do they have some other game in mind?

Playing the wrong game is more disastrous than playing the right game badly. Too many players accept, without question, the choice of game. The first lesson of *exploitation* is never to accept anything without question. In large organizations this means embedding a critical policy analysis unit at the heart of the business and endowing

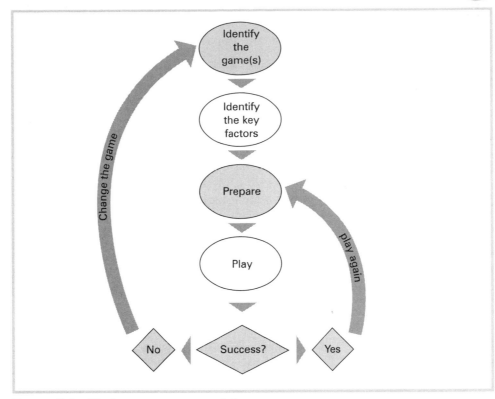

Figure 9.1 Playing a game successfully

that unit with high status and consequent respect. The unit must continuously review policy and continuously question the wisdom of staying in the game. It is most important that this process is continued during successful periods. Organizations become most vulnerable to the effects of game change when they are at their most successful. Success may breed success, but it also breeds arrogance and complacency. The dramatic fall from grace of Marks & Spencer, who remained oblivious to the fact that the retail game was changing, is a classic example. A high-status critical policy unit could have helped the company to stop digging once they had created their own hole.

playing the wrong game is more disastrous than playing the right game badly

This need to identify the games is also relevant within companies. Intra-organizational politics is even more complicated than inter-organizational game playing. Individuals, for example, will often hide their game intentions from others. Therefore, not only will there be a variety of obvious games being played simultaneously, but there may be others that are being deliberately concealed. It is up to the players to identify the hidden games as well as the more obvious games. This is clearly where intelligence is vital. 'Water-cooler' gossip, as it is called in the US, will generally illuminate the hidden games. It is vital that players continue to gather intelligence as a matter of course. The trap is the same as with inter-organizational games – success can breed complacency and laziness. Individuals develop a false confidence that their current knowledge bases are adequate for future games. Quite simply, they are dangerously wrong.

identifying the key factors

Which of the MORES are most significant – or are they all equally significant? It is at this stage that the interconnections of each element of the game become apparent. How *motivated* are you, for example, but also how motivated are the *others*? How *skil*ful are you and how *skil*ful are the others? How do you interpret and manipulate the *rules* and how are the others attempting to do the same? How can you deal with or alter the *environment* and how much will the others be doing the same? Games are dynamic because of the others who are also playing. Jean-Paul Sartre said that 'in football everything is complicated by the presence of the opposite team'. The same is true of business. No game takes place in a vacuum and the complexity of the situation is directly affected by the number of players. While you are updating your strategy, the others in the game will be doing the same – which means you have to make tactical and operational adjustments. It is the dynamism of games that makes them complicated and fascinating.

Another key factor is resources. Overwhelming superiority of resources can neutralize advantages in the MORES. However, it is just as important to recognize that resource superiority poorly utilized can be just as catastrophic. In modern business, where competition regulators are increasingly involved, no longer can companies indiscriminately use marketplace dominance to suffocate competition. That is not to say that it does not happen, but it takes greater skill and finesse to make it happen. It is the day of the foil not the broadsword. The modern weapon is a smart bomb delivered by a stealth plane and not blanket bombing delivered by hundreds of visible Lancaster bombers. In business and in most games, it is the skilful exploitation of resources that provides the competitive advantage, since resource levels are usually comparable.

preparing to play

Individuals, groups and teams all need to be prepared – and maintained – so that excellent performance can occur and continue to occur. If the policy analysis unit is in place it will provide critical analysis of the information gathered by the intelligence unit. As a result, the CEO and board will have identified the key factors of the game and generated the organizational objectives appropriate to the human and material resources at their disposal. The next task is to prepare the organization, at all levels, to play the game.

planning

The maxim 'failing to plan is planning to fail' remains true in many organizations. Where possible, the first preparatory task must be selection. It may not always be possible to select from a bottomless pool of talent, but the selection process is still vital to the success of any organization. The battery of psychometric tests and complex selection criteria have undermined, rather than enhanced, the selection procedure. They have provided a pseudo-scientific approach to what is an intensely human activity. What science is supposed to do in this quantitative approach is take out the emotion. It is precisely the emotion that should drive selection – not at the expense of reason, but as its companion.

Having selected a great team, the task then changes to one of maintenance. The manager must attempt to replace staff who leave with others who maintain the balance. Here, the 'big five' job performance indicators – extroversion, emotional stability, agreeableness, conscientiousness and openness to experience – are far more significant in the selection process than testing. These 'big five' are relative concepts – for example, what counts as extroversion in the civil service may not be considered so in the entertainment industries. Convergence between employer and employee, or manager and player will provide the balance that is the cornerstone of the selection process.

One thing that the modern business environment clearly has in common with football is the need to maintain a balanced team that includes star players on star salaries. This is especially true in the rarified atmosphere of the consultancy world where, according to Tom Tierney, the worldwide head of Bain & Co.:

Companies like ours are driven by stars. We compete for the top quartile of the talent pool. Those people have most of the options. You don't just have to recruit them, you have to keep them, which is often a bigger battle.

The star-player issue goes to the heart of the selection process. Can people be bigger than the team? The answer is no. People can be the biggest *in* the team but they cannot be bigger *than* the team. Being the star does not mean you are irreplaceable, because there are other stars out there. The team can continue to exist without you – it may even buy or develop a bigger star than you.

The same is true of managers. Selecting super-star CEOs is a precarious business, yet the ludicrous sums paid to head-hunting firms shows how organizations are prepared to outsource the acquisition of a core resource – people. Companies that would never dream of outsourcing other core elements seem happy to outsource the selection of key players. Remember, head-hunting firms are paid relative to the salary of the person they recruit, so it is in their interests to go for players with star salaries. In contrast, clever recruiters will widen and deepen the pool as much as possible. They will not deplete the pool by being ageist, sexist, racist or just plain bigoted; not because it is unethical but because it is inefficient. Good selection identifies people who at worst maintain the balance of the organization and at best enhance it. Selection is the most important element in the team-building tool box.

> good selection identifies people who at worst maintain the balance of the organization and at best enhance it

Talented people can succeed without coaching but coaches cannot provide success without the material. If an organization manages to combine the two – talented players and talented coaches – the potential is unlimited.

rehearsing the future

The next stage in the planning process is scenario planning – or rehearsing the future. In his book, *Sources of Power*, Gary Klein (1998) calls the process a 'Recognition-Primed Decision Model' (RPD). What Klein argues is that experienced decision makers do not actually compare options, they assess situations and judge them on a spectrum of familiarity. This enables them to evaluate alternative courses of action by visualizing how they would occur in reality. The decision makers effectively map future situations on to previously experienced situations. Decision makers make the majority of their decisions by recognizing that familiar situations are developing, or by recognizing that unfamiliar situations are developing – often referred to as 'expectation violation'. When expectations are being violated, decision makers are well advised to step back and wait for more information. If expectations are being confirmed, they will usually opt for the first, workable solution, which is not necessarily the best – they will 'satisfice' (Simon, 1957). Having selected the first option they will rehearse its implementation in their minds, analogously running the fast-forward on their mental videos, in order to 'see' any anomalies in the solution.

Figure 9.2 diagrammatically represents the process. What it does not show is the speed with which each phase is completed. In operational and crisis situations the process is virtually instantaneous, whereas with tactical and strategic decision making the process can take months or even years.

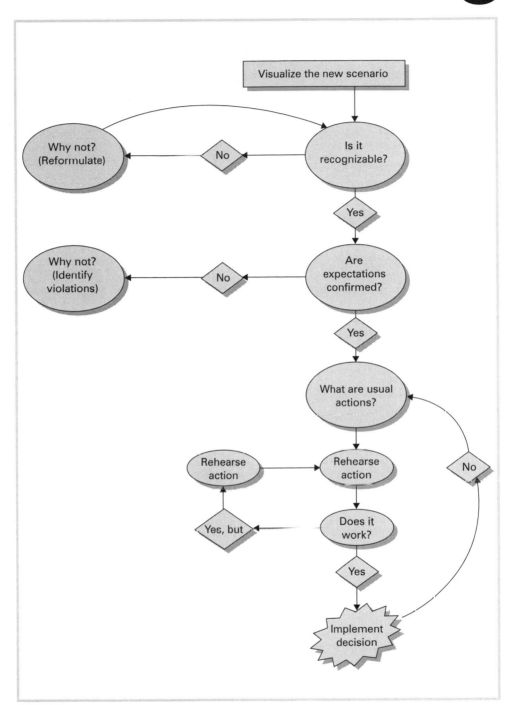

Figure 9.2 Rehearsing the future

resist or manage

In the business game, examples of how scenario planning can add value to the organization are innumerable. One of the most common is the 'resist or manage' scenario. In this scenario there is an expectation that an event or future situation is inevitable. Those who oppose the new scenario essentially have only two options, resist the changes or manage them. The big cigarette companies chose to ignore the inevitability of government intervention and huge litigation damages. In actuarial terms they were probably right, but a more sensible long-term approach may have been to emulate the alcohol industry, which has carefully managed its battle with the authorities to the extent that it has established an alcohol research institute, the Portman Group, and actively co-operates with government initiatives to suppress alcohol abuse. The smoking lobby, in contrast, has fought the authorities and pressure groups for so long that no goodwill remains. Individual companies have now begun the tortuous process of setting up individual deals with state and federal authorities in the US.

Railtrack is another organization that appears to have followed the tobacco model. However, the arrival of a new, more aggressive regulator, Tom Winsor, has resulted in heavy fines and terrible publicity. The bad publicity may cost Railtrack the London Underground contract, which had been all but signed and sealed. Railtrack's rehearsals had failed to account for a change of players. It was not alone. To anyone who had ever worked on a large-sale construction project with a tight time schedule the problems that befell the millennium projects were entirely predictable. Throughout 1999 a series of unofficial industrial actions, mostly by electricians, meant that prestige projects in London such as the Dome, the Jubilee Line extension and the Royal Opera House were under threat. Whatever the motives of the electricians, the situation in which an inflexible end-date was used to advantage should have been rehearsed.

There is a reluctance throughout British business culture to face the inevitable and manage it. This means that eventual compliance is usually gained on vastly inferior terms to those that might have been negotiated prior to a resistance strategy. In fact, resistance is generally a knee-jerk reaction that solidifies into a strategy as attacks upon the status quo increase. It is therefore all the more important for business players to rehearse scenarios at the earliest opportunity.

rule changes

Another common scenario that is under-rehearsed is that which deals with rule changes. There are obvious similarities here with the problems British industry has with the EU. Organizations are poor at recognizing when rules are about to change and consequently what those changes will demand. The Bosman ruling is a classic example. Even the most cursory reading of European law revealed the inequities of the contractual arrangements that pervaded football. The British football establishment simply refused to recognize the inevitable and many clubs lost players who could have been tied to contracts prior to the Bosman ruling. A head-in-the-sand approach is rarely the most advantageous to any organization.

The e-commerce world has already reached a point in which law making will critically affect its operational activities. But while trade is global, the law is mostly national. In the early days of new businesses it is the very lawlessness that actually attracts entrepreneurs. However, as the business arena matures, the players realize that legal certainty and consistency enables expansion of the market. At the beginning of the new millennium e-commerce finds itself at that very crossroads. Nobody is yet sure whose law governs in cyberspace. A non-governmental arbitration body, Icann (Internet Corporation for Assigned Names and Numbers), has been established to rule on domain name disputes. It applies the law of the jurisdiction it considers appropriate. Unfortunately, this remains a rare example of an effective arbitration body in cyberspace.

Business players need to be at their most adaptable to exploit the uncertainty in the law. They can do this in two stages. First, play both ends against the middle – operate in the spaces between the laws, but not outside them. In other words use the EU when it suits, then use Icann and so on. The battle between the EU and Bernie Ecclestone, the Formula One (F1) supremo is a case in point. The EU believed that commercial contracts between Ecclestone, the FIA (F1's governing body) and broadcasters contravened EU competition law. This news sent shockwaves through the financial world because it had just overseen the sale of £885 million's worth of Eurobonds issued by F1. Since the bonds were effectively underpinned by the TV contracts, the banks holding them were naturally nervous. Ecclestone and the FIA, however, were less nervous – because they had made contingency plans. Ecclestone had banked the proceeds in a family trust and the FIA had moved its HQ to Switzerland – out of EU jurisdiction. Ecclestone had played sensibly, the banks had played poorly.

business players need to be at their most adaptable to exploit the uncertainty in the law

Second, the players must position themselves for the scenario when it eventually settles down. This means rehearsing the future. Players need to explore avenues of rule avoidance and actively prepare for them with a series of alternative strategies. A clear example of a player aware of the difficulties was highlighted just before Christmas 1999 when Manfred Bischoff, the chairman of Daimler Chrysler Aerospace of Germany (Dasa), argued that continuing US regulations that limit technology sharing prevent transatlantic alliances. What Bischoff was doing was encouraging a campaign which he hoped would eventually force the rules to be changed. To this end he spoke worldwide at conferences and gave as many interviews as possible – he was preparing the environment. At the time of writing there are ongoing negotiations in the American political establishment about the retention of technology sharing restrictions. Bischoff, the player, had operated within the rules, but also tested their limits. He also positioned his organization to take advantage of any subsequent changes. All players should follow his example and remember the importance of rules, both stated and unstated. In particular, they should examine how much significance is attached to contracts, because they constitute the majority of rules in most modern business games.

preparing the environment

It is not only by anticipating rule changes that players can prepare for their games. For example, they can prepare the environment. In the business game preparing the environment is usually done verbally. The bombardment that softens the defences of the opposition come in the form of propaganda or spin. This is especially true in mergers and acquisitions. During Vodafone's attack on Mannesman, the Royal Bank of Scotland's on NatWest, and everybody's on Marks & Spencer, every 'real' move was preceded by a propaganda move. Disinformation can be deliberately leaked in order to disguise real intentions, or conversely genuine possibilities can be leaked to test the water.

preparing for others in the game

Players can also prepare for the activity of 'others' in the game. Most organizations, for example, are particularly poor at including personalities from public bodies in their planning. They recognize the existence of the post but do not investigate the individual who holds the post. For instance, a little more research by Railtrack on Tom Winsor may have paid dividends. Similarly, knowledge of the personalities of senior politicians is important for business players. Businesses rarely invest sufficient research time on the political and public policy areas until it is too late. Even if a policy analysis function exists, data concerning political issues is often ignored. Preparing for political changes should be an integral element of the preparatory process.

preparing for risk

The next rehearsal of the future is in the area of risk assessment and this is where gambling models are so useful. Gambling is the *model* for risk analysis and not an analogy. Risk analysis is not like gambling, it is gambling. The dynamic system that sets and adjusts odds in the betting industry is precisely the same as that which does the same job for stock markets, although the betting industry's procedures are probably a little more reliable. Both systems set the original odds relative to their knowledge of the players' performance potential. From that moment the odds (share prices) change according to the amount of money placed on each player and the amount of liability the odds-setters are prepared to bear. For more on this issue, see *Psychology of Gambling* (Bergler, 1985).

Central to rehearsing for the business game is the simple understanding that attitudes to risk will often decide an issue. In the betting industry we can see clearly who is risk averse and who is risk inclined – bookmakers are risk averse and losers are risk inclined. In business many players – Nick Leeson, for example – are caught up in the process of 'chasing your money', whereby gamblers initiate and continue a downward spiral to financial oblivion. As mentioned earlier, a gambling friend of ours uses the Bible to explain his attitude to risk: 'The race may not always be to the swift nor the battle to the strong [Ecclesiastes, 9:7] but that's where the smart money goes.' In the majority of cases, we would suggest following this advice.

preparing to be lucky

Luck is a topic avoided by most business books because it is difficult to quantify. Whilst it is difficult to explain, it cannot be ignored. And players can maximize luck: as Gary Player famously said, 'The more I practise the luckier I get.'

There are two tricks to making the most of random occurrences. The first is Gary Player's solution – practice. Players, in conjunction with coaches, have to select out successful skills and practise those. In that way they become prepared to take advantage of the luck that comes their way. The second trick is to recognize the opportunity that luck provides when it arrives. Only in Britain is the term 'opportunist' considered to be pejorative. In other countries opportunism is associated with talent. The key attribute needed to be opportunistic is alertness. Players, be they sports

> **players, be they sports people or business people, need to be alert to the unexpected opportunity**

people or business people, need to be alert to the unexpected opportunity. If, for example, a ball strikes the referee in football and drops into a player's path, that player must be able to see the opportunity (concentration), seize the opportunity (alertness) and exploit the opportunity (skill). Similarly in business, concentration, alertness and skill are the attributes needed to exploit random events (luck).

coaching for the future

The preparatory phase includes not only mental rehearsal of the future but also the physical preparation associated with coaching and training. The coaching and training processes must address the alternative scenarios that policy makers have only mentally rehearsed. The information gleaned from physically practising the future is an invaluable element of the feedback process and can save players from making mistakes that actually damage themselves or their teams. Whilst the advantages of preparation are obvious, it is often the first casualty in a recession. Yet it is precisely when the game is being played unsuccessfully that additional preparation and training are most required. Unfortunately, organizations usually reduce the training function when they find themselves under pressure.

The other main advantage of high-quality preparation is in the avoidance of crisis. Crises are generally considered to have three characteristics – surprise, lack of time to respond and a high level of threat. Sensible preparation can eradicate the first two of those characteristics and help players avoid crises.

playing the game

Ultimately, you have to play, prepared or not. However, preparation must continue while the game is in progress – there needs to be constant readjustment as the state of the game fluctuates.

Playing the corporate game is the task of *management*. Managing is not coaching; managers appoint coaches and provide the policy and strategic direction that coaches use as the template for their work. Managers are the CEOs, prime ministers, departmental heads, project chiefs, owners of small businesses. It is with the managers that the buck genuinely does stop. Managers manage people. In order to manage effectively, a manager must be able to do three things – make *decisions*, exercise *power* and *communicate*.

decision making

The decision-making process involves a recognition of previously identifiable scenarios. So the first stage in decision making is defining the situation. Decision makers view situations through their own perceptual lenses: they create a reality in which their decisions are rational. In the world inhabited by executives at Marks & Spencer (M&S), the company was, and always would be, *the* retailing giant and the model for others. Others, however, lived in a new world in which the values of M&S were outdated. For many years British industry ruled the world by sheer weight and quality of production in which a certain percentage of faults was viewed as acceptable wastage. Zero defect procedures and TQM destroyed that production philosophy.

It is the first duty, therefore, of decisions makers to analyze their own perceptions and compare them with the others in the game in order to minimize surprise. There is no such thing as a pleasant surprise in business. If you do not expect an event, then you are not managing well. Remember, too, that perceptions are not only individual. What is referred to as corporate culture is just another version of reality.

The second duty of the manager is to locate the decision at the right level. Is it strategic, tactical, operational or crisis? The position of the manager in the organization should coincide with the decision-making level. CEOs should delegate all decisions below the strategic. In a small business the levels may converge within a single manager, but generally the most senior manager should aim to delegate all but the most strategic decisions. Naturally if problems occur at the tactical or operational level then their relevant managers can seek confirmation, but it should not be obligatory to do so. 'Empowerment' is not just a force for improving morale – its greatest contribution is in terms of efficiency. As organizations grow it is simply not possible for one person to deal with decisions at every level.

Whoever is responsible for a decision, at whatever level, will have their own style of decision making, but there are still certain measures they should take to ensure a decision is implemented as effectively as possible. The trick is to involve all the individuals in the organization who will be affected by the decision – superiors, subordinates, peers, clients, suppliers and interconnected departments. Involving them has two significant benefits. First, they can add knowledge; second, they have ownership of the

the decision maker must not only bear responsibility, but must be seen to bear it by the others

eventual decision. The first benefits the process of making the decision, the second benefits implementation of the decision. Of course, involving people does not mean that the decision maker abrogates responsibility for the ultimate decision and its consequences. The decision maker must not only bear that responsibility, but must be seen to bear it by the others in the process.

power

The corollary of responsibility is power. There is no such thing as absolute power; all power is permitted by those over whom the power is exercised. While managers have the power to exclude players from the team, players have the power to refuse to perform (withdraw labour) or, more subtly, perform at a slightly lower level (work to rule). In either instance the power of the manager is diminished. It is, therefore, in the manager's interests to maintain the goodwill of the workforce. Sometimes, as with the electricians on the Jubilee Line, it is not possible to reach an accommodation because the workforce is mostly contractual and building a team culture becomes virtually impossible. In such instances a delicate balance between incentives and punishments has to be struck.

The balance of power is not about absolutes, but about the subtlety of distinguishing power structures. The Nokia group, for example, prides itself on its corporate culture. As its group president explained (*Financial Times*, 24 March 1999), 'Our corporate culture is one of the key contributors to meeting our ambitious growth targets'. The essence of the Nokia culture is viewed, by the president, as the abandonment of traditional management–worker relationships. Hierarchy is discouraged. Although hierarchies will always exist, either formally or informally, Nokia encourages its managers to transfer knowledge throughout the company – what Nokia calls 'competence investment'. However, Nokia's impressive growth means that more than half the workforce is made up of relative newcomers. As the careers of individuals begin to accelerate, stall or even decelerate, the goodwill of a knowledge-sharing environment will begin to leak away.

Research suggests that high levels of socialization tend to correlate with knowledge sharing. This is not good news for expanding companies. The socialization that is usually a characteristic of a small, start-up workforce will dissipate as the organization grows. Structures will drift towards hierarchy. It was interesting that the senior HR executive at Nokia illustrated the company's lack of hierarchy with the example of meetings of cross-functional teams: these were 'a chance for subordinates to tell managers what they think of

> it is how you manage the power accorded by the hierarchy that will distinguish successful management

them'. Where does the term 'subordinates' come from if there is no hierarchy? There is always a hierarchy: it is how you manage the power accorded by the hierarchy that will distinguish successful management.

However, some – possibly most – managers enjoy power for its own sake. And they are just as likely to be successful as are sensitive and empathetic managers. The most likely explanation is inappropriate managerial intervention. Perhaps Tony Blair *is* a control freak, but perhaps that is also why he so successfully manages the Cabinet. Perhaps they need controlling.

Managers have the power to intervene continually or very occasionally, or anywhere between. Management at a large consultancy will be minimalist and will mostly consist of initial selection and subsequent advice. A football manager, by contrast, will try always to keep a finger on the collective and individual pulses. Alex Ferguson has said that in management 'control is everything'. Ferguson's control is a product of the usual traits – he is a workaholic, obsessively concerned with detail, he values the team over any individual and he will not accept failure. However much the managerial texts might warn against such traits, they are the traits of all great corporate players. The chief operating officer of Korn Ferry International, Windle Priem, is not alone when he warns against listening to gurus who tell executives to work less and give more time to the family. He says: 'I've never seen a candidate's name cut from a short list because he or she works too hard. Successful executives do not permit themselves the illusion that their company's shareholders are eager for them to spend more time with their families' (*Financial Times*, 3 February 1999). The truth is that nobody really cares how successful players become that way, only that they continue to perform that way.

The greatest power that any manager possesses is the power to select. Again the crucial concept here is appropriateness. In his book on leadership, Julian Richer (1999), the chairman of Richer Sounds (the UK hi-fi chain), argues against recruiting 'super-talented whiz kids' because 'they are grass hoppers ... who hop to a rival firm for more money'. Richer goes on to say that he steers clear of rich kids and those with PhDs because he 'would rather take someone who may not have brilliant academic qualifications but is enthusiastic about the job'. Yet Tom Tierney of Bain & Co. says he wants the top quartile of the talent pool. What is appropriate to one organization may be inappropriate to another. When playing the game the manager must identify what type of personnel is required to achieve the objectives set out by the policy makers.

communication

Finally, if the managers are adept at making decisions and using, rather than abusing, their powers, they will need to communicate both to their staff and to other players in the game. Without good communication the best decision making and most powerful skills are useless. Communication is the art of selling ideas. Effective managers sell ideas to superiors, peers and subordinates. The guidelines are always the same (*see* Fig. 9.3).

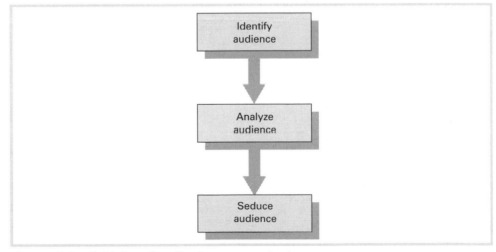

Figure 9.3 Guidelines for effective communication

Managers will often fail to *identify* precisely to whom they need to sell an idea, policy or decision. *Upwardly*, they may misunderstand who can veto an initiative. It may not be the ultimate decision maker and could be a gate-keeper. A powerful PA can block the transmission of your idea. On the *same level* they may ignore colleagues who have most to offer because they are from rival departments. *Downwardly*, they may fail to understand the support they will need at a later stage in the process.

Analyzing an audience entails acquiring a knowledge of their needs – understanding their fears, prejudices, favouritisms and motivations. The audience can then be *seduced* by pandering to those needs that the analysis has revealed – allaying fears, confronting prejudices, recognizing favouritisms and appealing to what motivates them. Get the communication process right and the rest will follow.

A report by RHI Management Resources (*HR Focus*, November 1999), indicated that the two most consistent mistakes companies make in managing their people are lack or recognition (19 per cent) and poor communication (63 per cent). Our own evidence suggests poor communication should be an even higher figure. In our coaching audit of the Virgin Atlantic ground staff at Heathrow we consistently heard stories about a lack of recognition. However, when we asked managers and supervisors about their staff they would often praise those very staff who felt undervalued. The problem was not that the efforts of staff were unrecognized, but that the recognition had not been transmitted to them by management.

Since communication is about selling, it raises the issue of transparency. We advocate transparency not for ethical reasons but for reasons of efficiency and effectiveness. It is inefficient to remain secretive for its own sake. The time, effort and resources needed to hoard information is phenomenal and, perversely, it indicates a lazy organization. The lazy way of dealing with information is to store it. The sensible way is to classify it and then either destroy it or disseminate it. This is true of both corporate and personal information.

Transparency also tends to be interpreted by others as an interest in people. Having a genuine interest in people is as essential for good communication as it is for good management. Those who are interested in people will be naturally good listeners – essential for good communication – and so natural repositories of corporate knowledge. It is, therefore, worth being transparent both for its intrinsic value and for the impression it creates

those who are interested in people will be naturally good listeners

of an interested management. Selling an idea is that much easier when the elements of fear and suspicion are absent, as they are likely to be in an open environment.

changing the game

The way in which players make decisions, exercise power and communicate will determine the degree to which they have exploited the game – how successfully they have played. If they have been successful they will re-enter the gaming process at the preparation stage (*see* Fig. 9.1). If they have been unsuccessful they must firstly carry out a complete analysis of every stage of their current game to ascertain whether they have performed to the maximum of their potential. This entails working through each aspect of the exploitation phase shown in Fig. 9.4.

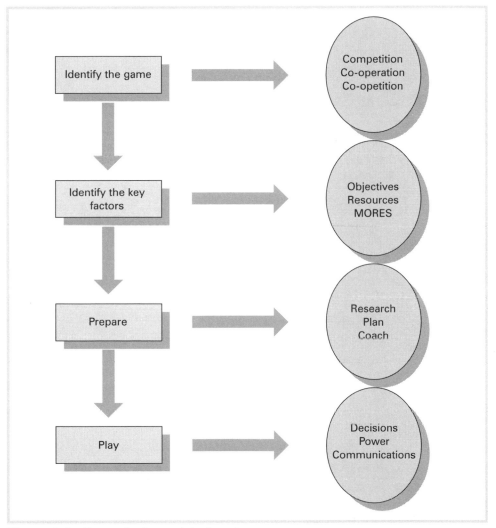

Figure 9.4 Stages in the exploitation phase

If players have not performed to the maximum, then deficiencies can be identified and corrective programmes put in place. If they have performed to their maximum and are still unsuccessful then they need to change the game or recognize, before anyone else, the way in which the current game is already changing. The reason for changing the game is simple. If you are not succeeding at the game you are playing, you must change or die. Of all the companies listed on the original Dow Jones Index in 1896 only General Electric has survived into the new millennium. Between 1975 and 1995 over 60 per cent of Fortune 500 companies were replaced. Compaq, which has replaced IBM as the largest PC maker, took just three years from its start-up to enter the Fortune 500; between 1991 and 1997 it transformed itself from a $3 billion enterprise into a $25 billion enterprise. In 1999 Marks & Spencer saw its profits fall for the first time in 30 years. The reason why giants fall – be they Goliath, the Roman Empire or extinct Fortune 500 companies – is that the innovative products or strategies that brought success are not those needed to maintain or recreate that success. What happens to organizations that fail is that they do not react to a series of forces that are acting upon them. The four forces for change are:

if you are not succeeding at the game you are playing, you must change or die

- *Copying* – the first threat to competitive advantage. In the modern business game new technologies are almost instantly copyable through reverse engineering and other techniques. This is why there are significant advantages in concentrating on process, because here the core competence is knowledge. Knowledge it is difficult to quantify and define and, therefore, difficult to copy.

- *Apathy* – accounts for the failure of companies to respond when their distinctive products or processes are copied. The greater the success of an original idea, the greater the resistance to abandoning it.

- *Obsession* – with a successful idea. Companies will push their original successful idea to breaking point. This is particularly common in technological companies, in which the 'techies' waste disproportionate amounts of their time improving the original product by a tiny percentage that provides little, if any, competitive advantage.

- *Success* – automatically changes the nature of the game itself. For example, the invention of mass production lines eradicated the production problem at a stroke. Markets were flooded with goods, which created a marketing game.

A good example of a changed game is the pharmaceutical industry. Here is an industry whose biggest companies regularly appear in the top five share-profit earners and who regularly post double the average profits of the FTSE 100. And yet, as Tom McKillop, CEO of Astra Zeneca points out, 'every pharmaceutical company has to reinvent itself on a ten-year cycle'. Why? Because the intellectual property rights of patented drugs only last, on average, ten years. After that date the production of generic drugs will kill the golden goose. As a consequence, the companies depend on a constant stream of new products. In the past the product stream was in the region of one new drug every two years. According to a report by Andersen Consulting (*Financial Times*, 1 June 1999) investor pressure is now demanding that the stream increase to five or six drugs per year – a ten-fold increase.

How can investors credibly demand such an increase? Because the game has changed. Firstly, the pharmaceutical industry used to be based on chemistry, but now it is based on biology. Advances in genetics mean that the number of biological targets that can be identified for research has increased exponentially. Secondly, the ability to synthesize chemicals through the use of robotics and computers has meant that millions of new compounds can be created in the time it used to take to create 100. Thirdly, data-mining software can match their databases against infinite numbers of targets. However, it is not simply the technology that has advanced. According to Sir Richard Sykes (Chairman of Glaxo Wellcome) there have been huge advances in the understanding of diseases rather than symptoms. That too will change the game.

To play the new game, two strategies are emerging – outsourcing and merging. Outsource too much, however, especially research, and you risk losing control. Merge, and the sheer size may kill creativity. To decide what is most appropriate for you, you must analyze the potential new games in relation to the MORES. Changing any game necessitates changing any or all of the MORES. If you feel that a change of game is necessary, then look at the elements that constitute the current game and identify those that can be changed. Changing even one of the MORES changes the essence of the game; changing them all makes it unrecognizable. And who will be able to beat you at a game they don't even recognize? But remember, if you can change the game, so can your competitors.

It is possible, therefore, to exploit the game by either perfecting the MORES of the existing game or by altering the MORES to change the game. The winning process is illustrated in Figure 9.5. For each element of the game there are key knowledge and key coaching issues. Ask yourself: what do you need to *know* about the MORES and what must you *coach*? Players who carry out this process can then *exploit* that skill when actually playing the game. If success still eludes you, then *change* the game.

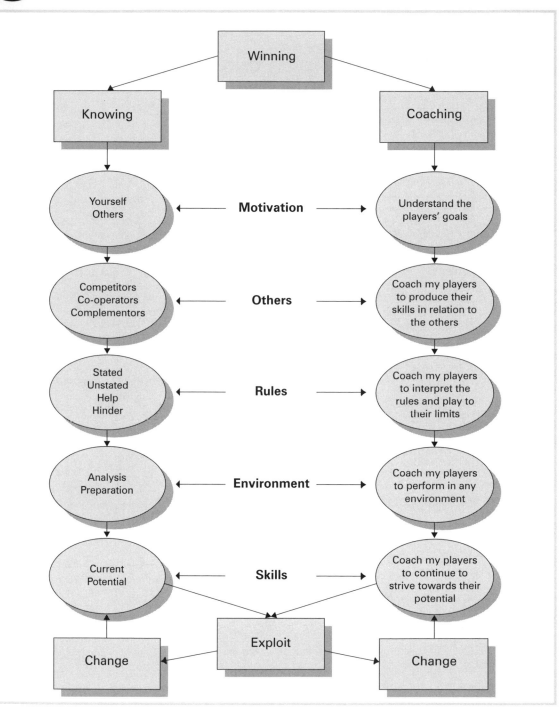

Figure 9.5 Winning the game

game plans

The brief case studies that follow originated in one month (April) in 1999 and were selected on the basis of high profile and contemporaneity. If you cannot recall the hot issues of that time, let us remind you. In sport it was, almost inevitably, Manchester United and its chase for the treble; in both the political and military spheres, Kosovo dominated the media. In business there were many cases vying for predominance and they included the BSkyB attempt to buy Manchester United, which made a nice link with the sporting domain. There was also the Microsoft litigation case, Marks & Spencer's crisis, and BMW's problems with Rover. Each provided a sufficiently different perspective on the corporate game to test the gaming model.

In each case we provide a narrative and highlight the elements of the game – the MORES. You will find a tear-out copy of the gaming model on page 136. Keep this with you as an aide-memoir and to enable you to add your own insights to the cases. We also provide marks out of ten for the main protagonists in the games. Compare it with your own evaluation. One small disclaimer – we realize that each case study could be a complete book in its own right, so we accept the apparent inadequacies of our interpretation. But even if there can be no one way of playing any game, there can be a right way of approaching the game. It's now up to you to make it your approach too.

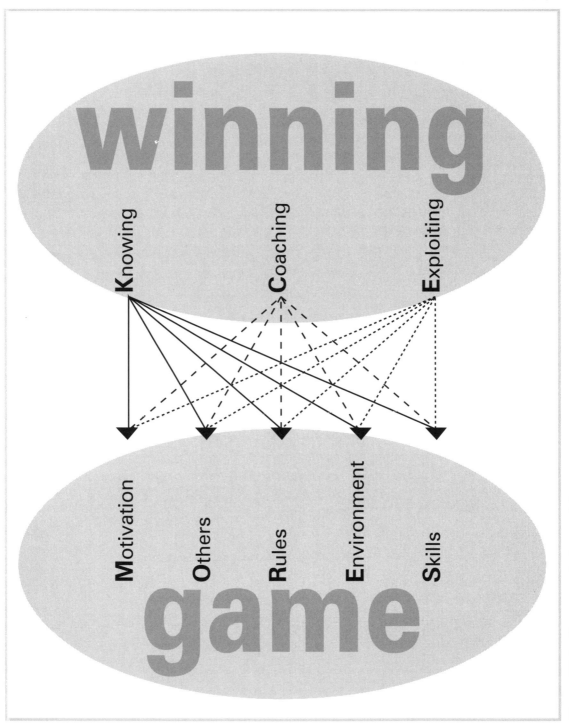

Figure 10.1 The game-playing model

the glory game

Manchester United and the treble

Whilst this chapter concentrates on the management of the footballing aspects of the treble chase, it is impossible to ignore the larger business game that Manchester United plc also has to play. For example, the game played between Alex Ferguson and Martin Edwards over access to funding was probably the most significant single factor in securing the treble. Funding for players' salaries and purchase escalated almost out of control in the final years of the last millennium and show no sign of abating in the next one. Ferguson himself argues that the £28.2 million purchases of Jaap Stam, Jesper Blomqvist and Dwight Yorke were essential if the European Cup was to be a realistic aspiration. In his autobiography, Alex Ferguson (1999) wrote: 'The treble was to be a seeming impossibility that became a reality but, looking back, I am sure that it would have remained just a plain impossibility had we not shaken off commercial caution and Stam, Yorke and Blomqvist.'

Ferguson makes an extremely pertinent observation about the uniqueness of the 'corporate' football game, stating that:

In the early summer of 1998 I had to assert myself on the need for Manchester United to spend money in the transfer market. For too long I had allowed the PLC to overwhelm me, accepting too readily all the City-speak about institutions and dividends and the harsh realities of the business world. It was time to argue with renewed vehemence my long-held belief that nobody invests more than the fans who pack [the] ground whenever we play there. They don't get a penny back and they are entitled to expect everybody at Old Trafford to demonstrate a desire to be the best.

For Ferguson, fans were not only stakeholders, in modern parlance, they were also investors. They are uniquely loyal – when was the last time anyone requested their ashes to be scattered in the aisles of the local Tesco? Mostly this loyalty is unshakeable, but as the directors of

Newcastle United found out, there are consequences. Their antics in Spain showed how a loyal customer base must not be taken for granted and should never be abused. The 'business' of football has to balance the demands of shareholders and stakeholders in a particularly visible environment.

Martin Edwards' 'game' was, therefore, increasing shareholder value. He was probably *motivated* by a combination of a desire to retain power and influence – giving him a status in the community – and the personal acquisition of greater wealth. The *others* in this game were his *competitors* (the other clubs and possibly Sir Alex), his *collaborators* (the other shareholders and possible partners, such as Rupert Murdoch) and his *complementors* (principally the media). The stated *rules* included the company laws, which apply to all businesses, and the competition laws, which would kick-in during the BSkyB negotiations. The unstated rule that seemed to dominate a great deal of Manchester United's corporate gaming in the treble season was that fat-cats are inevitable but there will always be an invisible limit to the fatness the rest of the players will permit. Success may breed success, but it also breeds antipathy. Of the cases we researched, the 'too fat-cat' rule is, perhaps, the most powerful and neglected.

success may breed success, but it also breeds antipathy

The *environment* in which Edwards was forced to play his game was one of unprecedented visibility. The Manchester United brand had become so powerful that the media focused permanently on Old Trafford. The *skills* he was required to demonstrate were in negotiations (with Ferguson, Murdoch and the government), diplomacy (the media, supporters and the government again) and, perhaps most importantly, in propaganda. Edwards needed to package and sell his vision in order to win his game.

During the season before the treble season Manchester United were the only Premiership club to register zero growth over the previous season: although their gate receipts increased, their merchandizing receipts were down. It is not clear whether this was the result of fan dissatisfaction or simply related to the general downturn in the retail sector and to sporting goods in particular. The point is that Edwards was not playing an easy corporate game just because Manchester United was number one. The other European giants, especially the Italian and Spanish, are catching up fast and the TV deals they are able to make individually may put them in the pole position in the not too distant future. If that day arrives, those United fans who played a part in resisting Murdoch may regret their actions. Of all the business domains professional sport is, perhaps, the one in which the concept of co-opetition is most apt. Intense competition is the norm, but without the presence of those competitors the entire business will cease to exist.

While Edwards was playing the corporate game, one of his employees, Alex

Ferguson, had other games on his mind. As Ferguson himself admitted, the European Cup had become the 'holy grail'. It was Ferguson's fifth attempt with Manchester United and 'reaching the semi-finals and the quarter finals in the past two years had sharpened [my] hunger to go all the way'. However, they had to pre-qualify because Arsenal had finished as champions of the Premier League the previous season. For Ferguson to cement his place in history alongside Matt Busby he had to win it – that was his *motivation*. The other competitions were important but secondary.

The *others* Ferguson was most concerned about were his *competitors* (Barcelona, Inter and Juventus primarily, although at certain stages he probably included Edwards on his list). His *collaborators* were his players and staff, although the loss of his Number Two, Brian Kidd, just before the quarter-finals revealed some misgivings Ferguson had harboured about Kidd's loyalty. Ferguson's *complementors* would be the teams that take part in the various competitions with little, if any, chance of winning. They can damage the chances of the genuine challengers by beating them in one-off situations.

The *rules* had gradually changed over the period of Ferguson's previous challenges. Teams were no longer limited to a certain number of 'foreign' players. This relaxation undoubtedly aided United. Also the league structure, as opposed to straight knock-out, had forced an alteration in tactical considerations. The unstated rule that was most significant was probably imposed by Ferguson himself: anything less than complete success is failure. This self-imposed demand for excellence could also be said to be the main *environmental* factor. Ferguson did not conceal his passion for the European Cup and in so doing increased the level of pressure on himself and his team. The tactical knowledge he and his competitors had gained about each other over the years, particularly with respect to Barcelona and Juventus, also made tactical surprise unlikely. Whilst Ferguson never subscribed to the common theory of continental superiority in technique, he did believe in a superior ability to stick to tactical game plans. His new coach, Steve McClaren, may well have been recruited primarily because of his reputation for tactical acumen and meticulous attention to planning and preparation.

The *skills* Ferguson employed most notably included resource management. Running a campaign, on three fronts, with limited resources looked like an impossible task. To appreciate the enormity of Ferguson's achievement, imagine being asked to bet on the treble when United were beaten 3–0 at Highbury in September; or when Keane was sent off in the FA Cup semi-final replay; or when Bergkamp

> the unstated rule that was most significant was imposed by Ferguson himself: anything less than complete success is failure

stepped up for a penalty in the last minute of the same game; or when Bayern twice hit the woodwork when 1–0 up in the European Cup final. The treble *is* impossible; the fact that United achieved it was mere aberration, a fissure in reality.

Ferguson managed his resources superbly. He had to integrate his new summer signings into a well-established organizational culture and indeed had some problems with Stam in the early parts of the season. However, all three signings added strength in the areas of United weakness. The signing of Blomqvist in particular emphasized Ferguson's determination to maintain the balance of the team even when Giggs was unavailable. Given the obvious importance of the Giggs/Beckham wide duo it was all the more surprising that for the final Ferguson chose to play Giggs on the right and Blomqvist on the left with Beckham in a central role. Ferguson's post-match rationalization of the contributions of Giggs and Beckham in their unaccustomed positions was just that – rationalization. In his book he admits that United were unable to reproduce 'the levels of fluency and penetration that had distinguished our best performances'. Despite their obvious superiority, United never looked like scoring for most of the match. The fact that they scored twice in injury time is a testimony to other Ferguson skills – team building, motivation and what Ferguson describes as the minefield of substitution.

There is no doubt that Ferguson's ability to forge genuine team-ness is his ultimate competitive advantage. The youth policy initiated immediately upon his arrival at Old Trafford is a testimony to strategic planning; the fruits of the planning – in the shape of Beckham, Scholes, Giggs, Butt, the Nevilles, Brown et al. – are there for all to see. 'My aim in management has always been to lay foundations that will make a club successful for years, or even decades,' said Ferguson. It is a maxim too often ignored in football and, perhaps more surprisingly, in business. His penchant for selection experimentation was compensated by the intense loyalty he shows to and receives from his players and staff. As he has said in his autobiography:

> ## Ferguson's ability to forge genuine team-ness is his ultimate competitive advantage

Tactics are important but they don't win football matches. Men win football matches. The best teams stand out because they are teams, because the individual members have been so truly integrated that the team functions with a single spirit. There is a constant flow of mutual support among the players, enabling them to feed off strengths and compensate for weaknesses. They depend on one another and trust one another. A manager should engender that sense of unity. He should create a bond among his players and between him and them that raises performance to heights that were unimaginable when they started out as disparate individuals. The Manchester United of 1999 had talent by the bundle but there was nothing about them that I admired or valued more than their team spirit.

General Sir Michael Rose, talking about his SAS troops, said that all the motivation and team-building work had to be done prior to an actual operation. Ferguson had done just that with the painstaking construction of the youth scheme, which is football's equivalent of the product development department. The foundations of the treble had been carefully laid in the early years of Ferguson's reign at Old Trafford.

assessment of the glory game

Ferguson's game playing is, perhaps, the easiest of our cases to assess because the criteria are so easily measurable. Did he win the treble? Yes. Were there lucky moments along the way? Yes. Does that matter? No. Ferguson pursued the holy grail and he found it. Now he has embarked on the journey once more, although there will be no treble this time because United did not enter the FA Cup, choosing instead to compete in the FIFA World Club championship in Brazil. Which brings us nicely back to the 'business' of football. Edwards gleefully accepted the invitation to go to Brazil as an opportunity to make brand penetration into a relatively barren market for Manchester United. It seems everybody is playing well at Old Trafford, irrespective of the game in which they are involved.

We award Ferguson 9/10 for his treble game. He does not get the maximum because a lack of discipline in his players nearly derailed the quest – the FA Cup semi-final dismissal of Keane and the absences from the European final due to suspensions. Manchester United also underachieved for 90 minutes of the final due to Ferguson's eccentric selection. (Of course, the main reason Fergie cannot be awarded full marks is that he is the manager of Manchester United – and 'we all hate Man U!')

Post-match analysis

At the time of writing United have retained the premiership and have been knocked out of the Champions' League by Real Madrid. Both outcomes were indicative of the strengths and weaknesses of Alex Ferguson. In the Premiership, his single-minded drive meant that there would be no let up in the champion's pursuit of another title; in the Champion's League his tactical adventurism finally came home to roost. However, perhaps the element of luck ultimately changed sides. Roy Keane's own goal was the flipside of the luck they had in the Nou Camp the previous year.

the expansion game

Manchester United and BSkyB

In early September 1998 news broke that Manchester United had accepted a bid of £625 million from BSkyB to acquire the public limited company. On 29 October 1998 the Secretary of State for Trade and Industry, Peter Mandelson, referred the proposed acquisition of Manchester United by BskyB to the Monopolies and Mergers Commission (MMC). On 12 March 1999 the MMC presented the new Secretary of State, Stephen Byers, with its report. On 9 April 1999 Byers 'announced to the Stock Exchange that in order to protect the public interest [he was] blocking the proposed merger between BSkyB and Manchester United' (DTI publication P/99/309). Rupert Murdoch had, it seemed, played the game and lost. But while Murdoch had indeed lost an element of the game, he is far from beaten overall. He may have lost a skirmish, but the battles and the war will continue.

BSkyB celebrated ten years of operation in February 1999 – confounding the sceptics who predicted a short and unhappy life back in 1989. BSkyB is 40 per cent owned by Rupert Murdoch's News International (Murdoch is also chairman of BSkyB), with the remainder of its shares held by institutional investors, including a powerful 25-percent holding by the French communications and utilities group Vivendi and BSB Holdings. BSkyB is at the forefront of the digital revolution and has invested heavily in this area, launching Sky Digital only four weeks prior to Mandelson's referral announcement. Sky Sports, one of BSkyB's three divisions, has been the main driver of the business. To use Murdoch's oft-quoted remark, 'We intend to use sport as a battering ram in all our pay-TV operations.' While it accounts for only approximately 30 per cent of BSkyB's revenues, Sky Sports, and the Premier League rights in particular, are central to BSkyB's strategic planning. Just as Murdoch's purchase, through Fox, of the rights to broadcast NFL football, had elevated Fox to number four of the national broadcasters, so too had the Premier League deal turned BSkyB from a no-hoper into the most profitable satellite-TV operator in the world. The failure of another Office of Fair Trading's (OFT) action against BSkyB, the Premier League and the BBC was cause for both celebration and concern in the Murdoch camp. Celebration, because it meant that its current agreement remained intact; concern, because it would now face powerful competition for the Premier League rights in 2001.

The acquisition of Manchester United was a strategic imperative that resulted from an overall objective to expand the Murdoch organization in the continental European market. Murdoch's penetration of the media/sports axis is well established in North America, where he either owns or has options to own super teams in the key sports of football, basketball and ice-hockey in the media centres of Los Angeles and New York. Expansion is seen by Murdoch as the best

expansion is seen by Murdoch as the best mechanism for the survival of his empire

mechanism for the survival of his empire. In order to expand BSkyB Murdoch needed to cover the two alternative scenarios. First, that the Premiership would be found to be acting as a cartel by the Restrictive Practices Court (RPC) and consequently clubs could secure separate deals; second, that the status quo would remain in place and consequently the TV rights to the Premiership would be up for auction in 2001.

The proposed purchase of Manchester United covered both bases. If the cartel was broken up then the new owners of Manchester United would be perfectly positioned to deal with *themselves* in designing programmes that would capitalize on United's huge popularity. If the cartel remained, this would also put BSkyB in the pole position in the auction for the new Premiership rights, because Manchester United gets the largest proportion of TV revenues (7 per cent). This means that a proportion of the amount BSkyB bid for the TV rights would come back to them in the form of Manchester United revenues. Consequently BSkyB would actually have an incentive to bid aggressively. Unless other bidders also bought clubs, they could not match potential BSkyB bids. Even if they did buy other clubs, the revenue-back would be less than that of Manchester United.

The problem that all the players had was that the RPC was taking so long over its deliberations. The case against the Premier League/BSkyB/BBC had been initiated by the OFT in 1996. When Murdoch made his move for Manchester United in September 1998 the RPC proceedings had yet to commence. The acquisition of Manchester United, therefore, made perfect strategic sense. However, by the time the RPC rejected the OFT's case in July 1999, Stephen Byers had already blocked BSkyB's purchase of United.

How would Murdoch have viewed the components of the game back in 1998? Murdoch is *motivated* by a desire to expand continually. He is driven not by money but by a need to consolidate and build his formidable empire. The *other* players in the game were diverse and made the game more complex than Murdoch appears to have imagined. Manchester United itself was never a serious player. Murdoch calculated, correctly, that the desire of the Manchester United board, and Edwards in particular, for personal fortunes would make their acceptance of the offer virtually inevitable. As for Murdoch's *collaborators*, he assessed, quite reasonably, that Downing Street would be his main ally. Number 10 would ease the path of any MMC deliberations. After all, Tony Blair had spent a great deal of time and energy in cultivating the media tycoon – having the backing of *The Sun* was considered essential during Labour's election campaign.

It is here that Murdoch miscalculated his bid. In the six months leading up to BSkyB's bid, Blair's populist stance as the people's defender of the people's game was being put to the test. Even the Fabian Society, Labour's left-wing think-tank, had produced a pamphlet that warned the government that it needed to protect the working-class game from the forces of commercialism that threatened its existence. The government had already established the cosmetic football 'task force' in response to the concerns of the fans for the soul of the game. The replica shirts rip-off, the fear of games on pay-TV, the price of tickets, the extortionate cost of 'refreshments' in the grounds – all these complaints were putting pressure on the supposedly fan-friendly Blair administration. Murdoch believed these concerns could be circumvented or even ignored. The politicians had no such luxury. New Labour was not, at that stage, in a position to distance itself from old Labour – and football was deep in the old Labour psyche.

At the height of these concerns Murdoch made his bid. Blair was, therefore, faced with charges of 'selling' the people's game to the ultimate people's enemy. Mandelson began making suitably neutral comments and Tony Banks, the Sports Minister, said that 'alarm bells' would be ringing in the corridors of power. It must have seemed to Murdoch that his main collaborator was about to jump ship. Ironically, Murdoch's *complementors* were other media companies such as NTL and Carlton, which were simultaneously his *competitors*. They registered interests in Newcastle and Arsenal respectively. Had such acquisitions proceeded then the monopoly argument against BSkyB may have been diluted. However, both NTL and Carlton waited for the outcome of the MMC investigation and this left BSkyB out on a limb.

Murdoch's really significant *others* were his *competitors* – and there were plenty of them. On the day the bid was announced, for example, the Supporters United Against Murdoch (SUAM) was formed and, combined with the Football Supporters

Association (FSA), it waged a powerful media campaign against the acquisition. They were aided and abetted by Murdoch's arch rival, the *Mirror*. The anti-Murdoch factor bound together disparate and apparently antipathetic groups – this anti-Murdoch factor was also the unstated *rule* that Murdoch either misunderstood or ignored. If, as the MMC ruling claimed, the merger would 'reinforce the existing trend towards greater inequality of wealth between clubs', then United fans should have welcomed

while it is permissible to be a fat-cat, you can't be too fat

it. Instead, they viewed it as the beauty of United getting into bed with Murdoch the beast. The unstated rule that Murdoch broke was the 'too fat-cat' rule: while it is permissible to be a fat-cat, you can't be too fat – don't take liberties.

Murdoch could be forgiven for being confused about the stated rules. These are the rules that govern mergers and acquisitions and competition issues. The process relies almost solely on the opinions of political appointees, with reference to the intangible concept of 'public interest'. In the first instance the DGFT (Director General of Fair Trading) assesses mergers that come to his attention (for example, through notification, press reports or complaints). One criteria for mergers to qualify for reference is whether the 'worldwide assets to be taken over are more than £70 million or a 25 per cent market share is created or increased in the UK, or a substantial part of it' (DTI regulations). The DGFT then advises the Secretary of State for Trade and Industry on whether to accept statutory undertakings in lieu of reference to the MMC. Both BSkyB and Manchester United made such under-takings, which were rejected on the grounds that the MMC 'did not find any that were regarded as effective'. In other words, they did not believe BSkyB and United. 'Evidence' was clearly unimportant.

Once the MMC has completed its deliberations, its report is submitted to the Secretary of State. If the report approves the merger then the Secretary of State has no further power to act. If the MMC recommendation is against merger then the Secretary of State has discretion either to block the merger or require the parties to the merger to satisfy certain conditions before permitting the merger to proceed. The Secretary of State is aided in this by the DGFT who acts as adviser on competition issues. So, the referral, the report and the decision are effectively the result of the opinions of the DGFT and the Secretary of State at particular stages of the process.

In this case we now know that Stephen Byers blocked the merger to 'protect public interest' although the actual ruling said that since the MMC were 'unable to identify any public interest benefits from the proposed merger … [it] might be expected to operate against the public interest'. On football matters the MMC found that 'the merger may be expected to have the adverse effect of damaging the quality of British football. This adverse effect would be more pronounced if the merger precipitated other mergers between broadcasters and Premier League Clubs'.

Our view, and that of other analysts, is the reverse. An editorial in *Management Today* (February 1999) prior to the MMC judgement explained the situation this way:

However unpalatable the pundits may find it, the proposed Murdoch take-over is a natural extension of a process that has already started. In the US and continental Europe, joint ownership of media and sports clubs is long established. The MMC should allow the deal.

Judgement of this case was clearly a matter of interpretation – opinion. And opinion was biased against BSkyB largely as a result of the Murdoch factor. At least one member of the panel was unwilling to refute the suggestion that the Murdoch factor had any bearing on the final recommendation and admitted that a special feature of the BSkyB referral was the 'substantial volume of hostile third-party interest'. The main problem with the Byers' decision was that it was a 'snapshot' decision. It failed to take into account the likely outcome of the RPC case and also the fact that other mergers between media companies and Premier League Clubs would not qualify for referral because no other club had assets in excess of £70 million or a 25 per cent market share. Byers admitted this inadequacy when announcing a 'wide-ranging consultation on reforming the mergers' regimes' to eliminate such anomalies. In fact, Byers later announced that the £70 million threshold would be removed and also that future decisions, except in very rare cases, would be taken by the expanded OFT or the Competition Commission. As Byers put it, 'business is entitled to know important merger decisions will not be influenced by short-term political considerations'. This was of little help to Murdoch, however, who clearly needed to pay far closer attention to the rules.

The same criticism can be applied to the *environment*. The mood at the time of the bid was anti-commercialism, anti-fat-cats, anti-messing with football and anti-Murdoch. Taking these issues more seriously would surely have generated a more environmentally sensitive approach to the merger – and possibly a more successful one. However, whilst Murdoch's recognition of environmental and rule issues was less than effective, his *skills* were perfectly suited to the longer expansion game he was playing. The skills required in such a game are both strategic and tactical, allied to a flexibility of approach. By using such skills Murdoch stayed ahead in the game. He expertly identified alternative scenarios that would enable BSkyB to continue to dominate the game, especially in its emerging digital format. He was helped by the RPC, which ruled against the OFT's contention that the Premier

League's practice of selling its TV rights on a collective basis represented a cartel. The RPC further concluded that the arrangement did not operate against the public interest. This ruling allowed Murdoch the breathing space to reposition BSkyB in the light of alternative scenarios. The most likely scenario now is that the Premier League will auction the TV rights in 2001 when the BSkyB contract expires. Murdoch's first move was to secure or obtain options for holdings in a variety of Premiership clubs. These included Manchester United, Leeds United and Sunderland – three of the Premiership's biggest clubs.

The Sunderland and Leeds deals revealed another Murdoch skill – deal making – since he paid additional sums to secure agents' right for both clubs. Although it took only a 5 per cent stake in Sunderland, BSkyB is now sole commercial and media agent for the Wearside club. BSkyB's bets were further hedged when £1.85 million of the total £13 million deal was made contingent on the club staying in the Premiership. Securing the same rights with Leeds cost Murdoch £4.6 million on top of the £9 million he paid for a 9 per cent stake in the club. BSkyB has also added Manchester City to its stable. BSkyB's alternative strategy for retaining the pole position in the race for the Premiership rights was to make an informal approach to the Premier League to negotiate a new three-year contract that would have run from 2000. This would have extended Murdoch's current deal by two years to 2003. His offer would have increased the earnings of the clubs by some 70 per cent over the life of the contract. Murdoch's approach was widely interpreted as the opening shot in the auction for the Premiership rights.

Another element of Murdoch's strategic positioning is the continental European dimension. He has already managed to secure 24 per cent of the German Kirch-Pay TV and is also courting Sogecable of Spain. However, the regulatory labyrinth of the EU is not an easy environment in which to operate. Also in Europe, another would-be partner, Canal-Plus, exerts a powerful influence over the market. Murdoch needs to be more sensitive in this market than he has shown in many others.

Finally, Murdoch has also recognized the environmental changes brought about by the electronic revolution and converging technologies. He appointed ex-BT executive John Brigewood as head of the new media aspects in November 1999. BSkyB's first online foray was a 5 per cent stake in Toyzone.co.uk, a toy retailer. It then went for a 10 per cent holding in Gameplay.com, the computer games group, and has also had talks with the Tote to co-operate in establishing an interactive

Murdoch recognized the environmental changes brought about by the electronic revolution and converging technologies

TV betting channel. This is a market where Murdoch's aggression would be asset because the competition will be fierce. The big bookmakers are now on-line, joining Internet bookies such as Blue Square and Sportingbet.com.

Competition is also strong in the sports/media business. Companies like Granada (which acquired a stake in Liverpool), NTL and Carlton have proved the invalidity of the MMC ruling and made this sector of the game a place for hard-ball players only. The battle with NTL will provide a severe test for Murdoch's skills. NTL is a £10-billion company backed by Microsoft, who injected £300 million into the company in 1999. NTL owns 9.8 per cent of Newcastle United and Aston Villa. It owns the network that broadcasts ITV, C4 and C5; it is in talks with Microsoft and Yahoo!; it sells Internet and other communications products over expanding cable networks; and with the acquisition of the Cable and Wireless domestic cable division it dominates the cable market. If the ultimate consolidation occurs between NTL and Telewest then BSkyB will have a battle royal on their hands. NTL alone is a formidable enough opponent, but it is rumoured to have struck a deal with Eurosport that will allow it to put together a £1-billion bid for the Premiership rights. The prospect of private equity firms entering the fray must be just as worrying for BSkyB, even though the Premier League is most likely to favour some sort of broadcaster.

assessment of the expansion game

Whilst many of the skills and activities we attribute to Murdoch are the work of his staff, in this assessment Murdoch must be viewed as the player, not least because he selects the staff and he is ultimately responsible. We award Murdoch 8/10, possibly moving up to 9/10 dependent on the outcome of the Premiership auction. The significance of sport is so great that failure to secure the rights would represent a significant defeat in the expansion game. Murdoch scores highly as a strategist and dealmaker. A 1999 Zenith Media report on the top 50 European media owners placed BSkyB at the top of the league when it came to exploiting assets (*see* Table 11.1) and also hinted at an eventual deal with Canal Plus that would elevate BSkyB to Number One in both leagues.

Murdoch scores highly as a strategist and dealmaker

Murdoch also recognizes strategic opportunities in a changing environment. However, on the negative side Murdoch can be insensitive to the demands of environmental issues, such as those generated by the fans in the Manchester United take-over. He can be overly aggressive and build up unnecessary animosity. BSkyB also showed a lack of sensitivity to the stated rules, and failed to realize the regulator was clearly influenced by the unstated 'too fat-cat' rule. Finally, and this can be both positive and negative, Murdoch is a nerveless risk taker. BSkyB very nearly brought News International down but Murdoch held his nerve. Will it hold in the next few years?

Table 11.1 The top media owners

Media groups' ranking			Return on assets		
Media revenue ranking		US$m	Media revenue ranking		% return on assets 1997/8
1	Bertelsmann	2965	1	BSkyB	32
2	CLT-UFA	2742	2	Channel Four	29
3	United News and Media	2694	3	Independent Newspapers	27
4	Lagardere	2522	4	Carlton Communications	21
5	Vivendi	2516	5	United News and Media	21
6	DMGT	2324	6	EMAP	17
7	BSkyB	2280	7	Axel Springer	17
8	Axel Springer	2276	8	Reed Elsevier	16
9	Reed Esevier	2197	9	Schibsted	16
10	Mediaset	1892	10	Scottish Media Group	15
14	Granada	1544	15	DMGT	13
18	Carlton Communications	1302	19	Johnston Press	12
19	Pearson	1108	20	Mediaset	11
20	EMAP	1088	21	Trinity	11
25	Independent Newspapers	908	27	Newsquest	7
26	Mirror Group Newspapers	848	30	Mirror Group Newspapers	6
27	Channel Four	842	32	Pearson	6
35	Trinity	561	33	Guardian Media Group	5
37	Guardian Media Group	535			
42	IPC	491			

Source: Zenith Media Yearbook 1999

Post-match analysis

As predicted, other media players such as Carlton, On Digital, NTL and Granada joined in the fray for the Premiership rights auction. They were joined by terrestrial companies keen to form alliances. As we now know BSkyB won the auction with a bid lower than that predicted by analysts and Murdoch therefore retained his 8/10 status.

the dirty games

NATO and Kosovo

Our interviewees readily identified with the game concept in relation to Kosovo. Yet of all our cases it is the most difficult to delineate precisely, because there were so many separate and sub-games being played. So this chapter deals not with a single game but with a multiplicity of games. We will examine four separate but interconnected games. The first is what might best be described as the 'civil war' game: the attempts by the various groups within the former Yugoslavia to either consolidate or expand (or both) their territorial claims. It was in this game that ethnic cleansing was used as a strategic ploy towards achieving the overall objective of a secure, stable and 'pure' Serbian nation-state. It is not a new game – as Northern Ireland, Vietnam, Cambodia and sub-Saharan Africa clearly show – and neither are the tactics of ethnic cleansing and genocide – the settlement of Africa, the Americas and Australia are classic examples of the worst excesses committed in the pursuit of a national identity.

The second game is the 'humanitarian war' game. This is a relatively new game and one that has proliferated since the end of the Cold War. Between 1945 and 1988 there were 13 official UN peacekeeping or peace-enforcement operations and one UN war (Korea). Since 1988 and the establishment of a single superpower, there have been at least 37 operations and another war (Gulf). 'Humanitarian war' has come to mean those conflicts that are fought by external powers and coalitions in the cause of humanitarian relief. They have become the enforcement equivalent of humanitarian aid, with the objective of relieving suffering.

The third game can only be described as the 'remnants of the Cold War' game. In this game the players play familiar roles they have transplanted into an unfamiliar environment with unfamiliar rules. For example, while the antagonism between Russia and the USA remains, the balance of power has significantly altered. What this has produced is familiar posturing but unfamiliar solutions. The fourth and final game is the 'internal' game. That is the political game played within the boundaries of each of the organizational players. While the internal games were primarily self-contained, they were still connected to the internal games being played by the other players. Although Milosevic, for example, may have been indifferent to the suffering of Kosovar Albanians he could not ignore the impact the suffering was having on the governments around the world as a result of their domestic media pressure. The inter-connectedness of the various games is a dominant feature of the Kosovo game.

game one – civil war

The apparent *motivation* of virtually every player in the civil war game was an historically rooted xenophobia. The constant references, by all parties, to the short, medium and long-term past all pointed to a deep-seated fear of ethnically differing groups. The Bosnian civil war had re-alerted observers to the depth of animosity that existed in the Balkans, but Kosovo still came as a surprise. However the motivation was presented to the outside world – as survival, stability or security – it can only really be explained in terms of xenophobia. The *others* in the civil war, seen from the Milosovic viewpoint, were primarily competitors and collaborators. The *competitors* were the Kosovar Albanians, particularly the KLA. The *collaborators* were the Russians. The *complementors* were all those who were prepared to stand by, which initially meant most of the world. One of Milosevic's tactical failures was in antagonizing the great powers – to the extent that he managed to convert them from complementors to competitors.

The unstated *rules* were relatively simple – keep other states out. In civil wars there are no stated rules. By their very nature they represent a rejection of previously stated rules. The geographical *environment*

in civil wars there are no stated rules

was important because the unhospitable terrain meant that external interference was likely to be slow and reluctant. The political environment, at least internally, was sufficiently stable and supportive to encourage Milosevic's adventures.

The *skill* set required in a civil war includes aggressive prosecution and strong unwavering leadership. The leader also needs to have a political sensitivity in order to keep other states out of the conflict. Here, Milosevic was particularly weak, although he was a master of brinkmanship and did recognize weakness when he saw it. His own weakness was that he did not recognize strength of resolve when he saw that. Milosevic's main competitors, the KLA, understood both strength and weakness – their own and others. They worked hard to involve external states and utilized their main weapon – guilt – expertly. They had extremely limited resources and yet managed to ensure their survival and indeed legitimacy, to an extent nobody imagined. The other players, the Kosovar Albanians, lost on all counts. They were dispossessed, disenfranchized and exiled. In many instances they were killed – the ultimate losers. Whether or not they could have played their game much differently is a moot point – in civil war games the people are also just pawns.

assessment of game one

Milosevic scores 6/10. He achieved most of his objectives, but poor tactical judgement invoked the anger of powerful players, who may well remove him from the game completely. He showed strong leadership and aggressive policy making. He was quick to spot weakness, but slow to recognize strength in others. The KLA, by contrast, must be awarded a strong 8/10. They knew their limitations in both resources and influence and utilized them to the fullest extent. Where they failed was in fully exploiting the support of the West against Milosevic. Once the NATO campaign had halted Milosevic, the KLA immediately engaged in reprisals that alienated NATO support. They did not recognize that the game for NATO had more dimensions than the civil war. Nevertheless, they still managed to convert themselves from guerrilla paramilitaries to legitimate players during the process of the game – a major success. As with all wars the only complete loser was the general populace; as usual they score 1/10 because they never even agreed to play the game. Their problem was, of course, a negligible resource base. Pawns and foot-soldiers may be essential to any game, but they are also expendable.

game two – humanitarian war

Humanitarian war is a new type of game. It is a kind of war with which most of the players were unfamiliar. Inter-state war, civil war, guerrilla war – such conflicts were well-established modes of activity for the players. In contrast, armed forces fighting wars driven by altruism was an unlikely scenario. When NATO's planes took to the skies on 24 March 1999, it was at least in part the result of high-blown rhetoric. Words *are* deeds: when President Bush uttered the words, 'Watch my lips, no more taxes', it became a deed. It tied him irrevocably to massive budgetary scrutiny. Similarly, in Kosovo the NATO rhetoric of humanitarianism tied it into inevitable action.

It was this pragmatic humanitarianism that provided the primary *motivation* for the NATO governments, especially those of the UK and the USA. Both governments were ultimately driven by the 'don't just stand there, *do* something' mentality, which saturation media coverage generates. In a Channel 4 programme, *Europe at War*, the US Special Envoy to the Balkans in 1998, Richard Holbrooke, explained how the horrific picture of a dead Kosovar Albanian, which dominated the front page of the *New York Times*, had affected the mood of a White House meeting on the issue. Holbrooke said: '*The Times* sat in the middle of the oak table in the middle of the situation room and had a very real effect on the dialogue.' Once into the conflict, NATO was motivated by pride. As Henry Kissinger put it (*Los Angeles Times*, 13 April 1999), 'Once in, NATO's credibility [was] on the line.' Ten days later Tony Blair reiterated NATO's commitment when he said that 'Success [was] the only strategy [he was] prepared to consider.' Both statements smack of the sunk-cost fallacy.

The media is a powerful influence and the 'don't just stand there' syndrome also affected some of the *other* players such as the UN and the various non-governmental organizations (NGOs). Russia, the KLA, Milosevic and the media, although not motivated by humanitarian rhetoric, were still aware of its power in the other camps. NATO's *collaborators* were primarily the other members of the UN Security Council who legitimized NATO's actions. NATO's *competitors* shifted between Milosevic and the KLA. As each gained some level of ascendancy they wished NATO to back off. However, Milosevic was clearly NATO's main competitor. The *complementors* were more difficult to identify. They included the NGOs, the media (who were also often perceived as competitors) and, directly linked to the media, domestic public opinion.

Closely related to the motivational imperatives were the *rules*. For NATO these were simple. Stated rules, that is international law, had to be adhered to and if transgressed had to be answered. NATO consequently spent much of its time apologizing or justifying the bombing civilians, radio stations and most embarrassingly the Chinese Embassy. However, these 'mistakes' were overridden by the primary unstated rule – 'you can't do nothing'. For Milosevic and the KLA, however, there were no stated rules. The unstated rule was 'get as much as you can' without antagonizing NATO too much. This imperative to act ran through the whole Kosovo situation as far as NATO was concerned and was largely *environmentally* driven. The significant environmental factor was blanket media coverage. Within 48 hours there was virtually complete transparency. Secrets are hard to keep at the best of times, but in the modern environment the CNN factor

> 'mistakes' were overriden by the primary unstated rule – 'you can't do nothing'

makes it impossible. The local geographical environment was also less than welcoming and had a large bearing on the tactics. Every NATO state was reluctant to commit ground troops in such an inhospitable terrain. At no stage, for example, was Congress going to support the use of ground troops and President Clinton, in the middle of the well-known Lewinsky game, was in no position to fight them.

Without the possibility of ground troops the *skills* required to succeed in the humanitarian war were fairly clear. They were primarily the political skills of leadership and propaganda. Both Blair and Clinton were politically astute, even though this was Blair's first major foreign policy adventure. Where they failed was in being sufficiently forceful as de facto political leaders of NATO. Because of their inability to convince their domestic audience of the need for casualties, they deprived the military of the necessary resources to win the humanitarian war. In a lengthy interview we conducted with General Sir Michael Rose, who commanded UNPROFOR in Bosnia in 1994, he argued that NATO actually played the wrong game. This was because, he said, they failed to learn the most important lesson Bosnia had thrown up – that 'you can't solve complex, political or humanitarian problems from the air'. He opined that 'the decision to announce publicly that NATO would not deploy combat troops in an offensive role allowed Milosevic the freedom to launch a full-scale pogrom of the Kosovar Albanians'. The consequence was, of course, that the aim of the NATO campaign, which was to 'prevent more human suffering and more repression and violence against the civilian population of Kosovo', remained unfulfilled. So, according to General Rose, NATO leaders were forced to play the wrong game as a result of their own inadequacies.

A leader in the *New Statesman* (9 April 1999) put the political imperatives in a nutshell:

The 'something-must-be-done' school prevailed. NATO's reputation, the moral comfort of western peoples, the political virility of their leaders, the mission to teach tyrants a lesson – all these took precedence over sensible strategic calculations or for that matter, the welfare of the Kosovan Albanians.

If the criteria listed by the *New Statesman* as objectives are accurate then the NATO strategy might well be said to have succeeded.

NATO was also forced by its lack of understanding to employ that other partic-ularly relevant skill – propaganda. The fact that in Britain the most recognizable face, other than the relevant Cabinet ministers, was that of Jamie Shea indicates how significant propaganda is in these situations. Many argued that it became the dominant tactic in the prosecution of the war. A vivid example occurred when NATO planes mistakenly attacked a civilian convoy. Blair's response was to despatch not a senior military adviser but his press secretary, Alistair Campbell, to NATO high command in Brussels. Blair's first reaction was to 'spin'.

NATO was eventually able to claim victory and argue that Milosevic withdrew his troops from Kosovo as a direct result of the air campaign alone. It can also claim that the refugees were returned home. However, its original aim was not achieved; there *was* a humanitarian disaster. J.K. Galbraith once noted that government is generally a choice between the disastrous and the unpalatable – both Blair and Clinton chose the disastrous.

assessment of game two

We awarded 7/10 to all the major players in game two because they all achieved the majority of their real aims, as opposed to their stated aims. NATO *did* something and sustained no casualties. Clinton diverted attention from his Lewinsky game and Blair looked like a statesman. Milosevic slaughtered a huge number of Kosovar Albanians and remains in power at the time of writing. The KLA transformed itself from a Balkan IRA to a Balkan ANC. The media filled its pages and screens and the NGOs paraded their humanity. The UN, as usual, performed its role of scapegoat, which allowed the other players to portray themselves in a favourable light. The losers? The losers were the ordinary Balkan people.

game three – the Cold War leftover

Game Three was an interesting sub-plot to the main game. The old adversaries of NATO and Russia retained a distrust of each other and a need to assert themselves. Russia was *motivated* by pride, which had been seriously dented since the end of the Cold War. However, the parlous state of the Russian economy meant there had been little opportunity to defy American power. The Kosovan conflict provided such an opportunity. *Izvestia*, the Russian daily, explained how the NATO bombardment had given the left of Russian politics a priceless gift – a common enemy. That enemy was the most significant *other* in the game, even though all the old allies still had their part to play. Despite the pleasure of tweaking the American's tail, the Russians had to remember the *rule* that continued to apply in the Cold War game – no inadvertent escalation. In the post-Cold War *environment* it was not too difficult to abide by the rule. Everybody realized that Russia was in no position to escalate and the *skill* the Russians had to employ was that of the brinkman irritant. They knew they would be needed in any negotiations and played on the situation in order to reassert themselves on the world stage.

assessment of game three

Both NATO and the Russians score a respectable 7/10 for their reprise of the Cold War game. NATO established its pre-eminence as the only credible military agency in Europe. The clamour for an EU force had been dissipated for a while. However, the failure of NATO to achieve its original aims limits its score. Russia managed to achieve its aim of re-establishing itself as a world player, but could never score maximum points because it never had the resources or political muscle to achieve the pre-eminence it once enjoyed.

game four – the domestic political game

The domestic political game played by each participant has been touched upon in the previous sections. Clinton was being 'Lewinsky-ed', Blair needed some *gravitas* and Milosevic needed to reassert his nationalist credentials. They were all *motivated* by personal political imperatives: Milosevic to stay in power, Blair to consolidate power and Clinton to put a mark down for posterity. The significant *others* were mostly *competitors* – internal political opponents. The *collaborators* consisted of external support, such as the Russians for Milosevic. *Complementors* were the media and the NGOs who enabled the internal political game to be carried to the people. In Britain and the USA the influence of the media was a suppressant, whereas in Serbia the media was an arm of the Milosevic government. Internal politics, in the West especially, has a simple rule that seems to be 'never be frank' – its too dangerous.

The *environment* was again the glare of publicity. In political terms the media are an ever-present environmental factor. The *skill* set needed was that of the snake-oil salesman. Milosevic had the easiest job because a siege mentality enables leaders to bond their populace behind the edifice of nationalism. Clinton had the most difficult task because of the relentless pressure he endured over the Lewinsky affair. Blair had to be careful, but he was relatively bullet-proof because of the virtually non-existent opposition in the wake of Labour's landslide victory in the general election.

media are an ever-present environmental factor

assessment of game four

Milosevic only scores 7/10. At one stage he had played a close-to-perfect game; however, he genuinely misinterpreted the determination of the West to prosecute an humanitarian war. Blair scores a healthy 8/10 because he emerged from the experience relatively unscathed. He played the concerned statesman game almost to perfection, but he was ineffective in terms of the type of leadership needed to achieve NATO's initial aims. Clinton scored low on the internal game – a weak 6/10 – because of his miscalculations over the Lewinsky affair. He handicapped himself in his dealings with Congress and thus in his ability to use the Kosovo conflict to enhance his domestic standing. While his showing was competent for anyone else, it was weak by his own standards as the consummate political player. Clinton was driven by two motivational factors. He had an insatiable appetite for campaigning and he wanted a place in history. Although he satisfied both, the latter was not in the manner he would have wanted. Clinton's score is bench-marked against his own previous performance.

The interconnectedness of the four games gives you a feel for the complex and interrelated nature of gaming in the international arena. Politics, diplomacy, military strategy and tactics are all there. And the number of references in the media as to whether Milosevic and/or NATO was bluffing was pure poker language. The Kosovo game was played out – and is still being played out – by some accomplished gamers.

Post-match analysis

Nothing much has changed – NATO politicians are still playing with the lives of people in far-off places and local politicians are playing with the lives of their own countrymen. The Balkan game may never end.

chapter 13

the crisis game

Marks & Spencer

In the first quarter of 1998 sales by Marks and Spencer (M&S) were particularly strong. In response, it stocked heavily in readiness for the autumn/winter season. At the same time consumer activity in the fashion industry was waning. M&S missed the signals and in the final quarter of 1998 experienced the largest year-on-year decline in sales since 1992. M&S was hit especially hard because its purchasing policy makers had disastrously misread the market and alienated an important segment of its customer base, young women. The culmination of these factors forced a huge winter sale in order to shift the stock. The sale meant that M&S sacrificed profit margins, which compounded the poor early season sales. M&S explained the collapse on the selection of black and grey as its dominant fashion colours for the season. Six months later the finance director was blaming 'exceptionally warm weather in the first half of September [for] deferring normal autumn purchases' and using this as an excuse for M&S's second profits warning in less than a year.

Black and grey may well have missed the fashion boat but it did not help that lines were already overpriced, primarily due to M&S's traditional practice of localized purchasing. At least 65 per cent of its clothes were purchased from UK suppliers. M&S itself blamed the strength of sterling for the overpricing. Yet this did not seem to be affecting close rivals BHS and Debenhams. Despite its protestations, M&S had clearly lost its way. It had failed to update its store layout and design, there was a chronic lack of personnel to attend to customers (particularly in the changing areas) and there was an outdated concept of service. All these alienated the customers. There was also a very visible boardroom row concerning the succession to Sir Richard Greenbury, the retiring chairman and CEO. The pre-game favourite Keith Oates was ousted, after an unsuccessful coup attempt, and the betting underdog Peter Salsbury took over as CEO. M&S then took over a year to find a new chairman. This alienated the city and shareholders became jittery. The concern of the shareholders was exacerbated by the £3-billion capital-spending programme initiated to expand M&S's sales area by 10 per cent (this included the purchase and consequent integration of 19 Littlewood stores). Unfortunately, the increase of sales area coincided with a 4 per cent decrease in sales in the crucial Christmas run-up and post Christmas sales. The Christmas problems merely accentuated the fall in first-half profits by 24 per cent. As a result of the pre-Christmas débâcle, full year profits showed a drop of nearly 40 per cent over 1997. The decline in share price precisely mirrored the profit gloom. At the beginning of 1999 M&S shares were at 333p against a peak of 665p in the final quarter of 1997. It was getting to the point where M&S was being viewed as a vulnerable take-over target for the gathering predators.

This was the situation that the new CEO, Peter Salsbury, inherited in January 1999. M&S was vulnerable, outdated and inflexible. Its stock was overpriced, unfashionable, poorly purchased and black and grey. The management structure was unwieldy, unresponsive and poorly structured. Most importantly, shareholder value was plummeting. Salsbury responded in

M&S was vulnerable, outdated and inflexible

a variety of ways, but they all smelled of panic and appeasement – they were not targeted at the underlying problems. One of Salsbury's responses was an attempt to modernize the antiquated supply chain and highly layered procurement system. This move entailed ditching some traditional suppliers, such as William Baird (a supplier for 30 years), in a bid to bring down costs by importing a greater proportion of clothing from cheaper overseas markets. It also entailed streamlining the actual chain itself. Traditionally M&S has used Britain as a hub for supplying its stores. This meant goods made in India bound for Hong Kong stores would be flown West to Britain in order to be shipped back East to Hong Kong. Streamlining this procedure had the advantage of shortened time-lags since shelf re-stocking could be reduced to 72 hours. Such flexibility should enable the disastrous overstocking of 1998 to be avoided in future. Salsbury's other responses were to authorize additional expenditure and focus on e-commerce and Internet advertising. He also reduced training expenditure to the extent that M&S cancelled its 1999 graduate trainee programme and withdrew consequent job offers. It also flirted with the idea of selling and leasing back some of its high-street stores in order to generate cash to spend elsewhere. It even considered leaving the peppercorn-rented haven of its HQ at Baker Street.

However, potentially the most radical response was to restructure completely the upper management echelons. The structure itself was altered, so that the company split itself into seven business units in an effort to improve its customer focus, and changes were also made to personnel. The seven unit leads, for food, women's, men's, lingerie, children's, home and beauty, all report directly to the CEO and all units will be fully profit-accountable. The personnel changes were, perhaps, even more significant. Alan McWalter, the new marketing director, got the key role. As he himself pointed out: 'If you look at any of the great brands … marketing pervades the organization. My job is to instill a marketing ethic and a marketing process within M&S' (*The Sunday Business*, 26 September 1999). Traditionally, M&S has never needed to lever the brand and has consequently been more concerned with quality of goods than quality of service. Astonishingly, until quite recently M&S did not even have a marketing department. McWalter aimed to change that. Perversely, his opposition came from within the Baker Street HQ. McWalter's immediate predecessor, James Benfield, had been a highly regarded long-serving (29 years) M&S man and his culling by Salsbury caused some concern at Baker Street. However, McWalter enjoyed the backing of the CEO – at least, initially. The other crucial appointment was to give Clara Freeman the 'UK stores' job in addition to the personnel brief she previously held. The retention of the personnel function, combined with stores, was another signal of a new customer-driven strategy. Although the role was welcomed by analysts, there was some concern that a relatively unknown insider had been chosen. Her impact has yet to be experienced by the customers she so wants to court.

Overall the executive team has been slimmed from 21 (plus six non-execs) to 14 (plus five non-execs) under Salsbury. Salsbury effectively stripped out a complete reporting layer in an attempt to facilitate speedier decision making. Salsbury also cut 400 HQ jobs, cut back on European operations and pulled out of Canada completely. He divided the company divisionally into British retail, overseas and financial. All this restructuring, however, failed to achieve the genuine 'bottoming-out' Salsbury spoke of in May 1999. In the *Financial Times* (19 May 1999) Salsbury said: 'We have bottomed-out. We have taken the first steps to recovery and we are starting to work on growth.' Following that statement M&S shares rose 20p to 399p. Nine months later in February 2000, they stood at 269 – despite the eventual appointment of a new chairman.

The new chairman received a £2.2 million 'golden hello' and a package that could earn him in the region of £15 million over five years, if he survives that long. Luc Vandevelde was formerly the MD of French food retailer Promodes, which throughout the 1990s was the best blue-chip performer on the French stock market. The way Vandevelde and Salsbury play together will be a crucial factor in the future of M&S. Whether Vandervelde is the person 'who will challenge every assumption and [be] an alter-ego for a management board that is largely inbred', as Mike Prefontaine of Arthur Andersen hoped for, is open to debate. If he is not, then Salsbury alone will not have sufficient strength to lever the tiller.

Identifying the game's MORES is especially complex in crisis situations because once a crisis has been identified, the game and its MORES change. As a consequence each factor will be examined in two phases – before the crisis and in the crisis. *Motivation* is a good example. Prior to the recognition of the crisis situation, M&S was motivated by a smug desire to maintain its superior notion of dignity. The disdain with which senior management looked upon credit cards, for example, was illustrative of their general complacency. They were in a warm comfort zone and had no desire to leave it. They were motivated not by a desire to satisfy the requirements of their fiduciary duty to their shareholders, but by a desire to retain the status quo. Once the severity of the crisis was realized their immediate motivation became survival, although in the long term they also wished to retain their own positions. They awoke from their slumbers and tried to adopt a more pro-active and customer-focused culture.

once a crisis has been identified, the game and its MORES change

They finally recognized that there were *others* playing the game – competitors, collaborators or complementors. Observations of their supply chain indicate that M&S rarely, if ever, reviewed the contribution of their 'big four' main suppliers and felt comfortable with the relationships. They were blissfully unaware of the level of the challenge that *competitors* were mounting on their core business and their competitive advantages. On the clothes front there was mass-marketing of designer labels such as Calvin Klein and Ralph Lauren at prices only just above St Michael's prices. Debenhams, Next, Gap and French Connection had filled the middle market and Asda's George range had proved a huge success at the lower end of the market. On the food front the big four supermarkets were cutting into the premium quality prepared-food niche that M&S had taken for granted as theirs. There was also the convenience of out-of-town superstores. Why carry food home from a town centre M&S when you can drive home from a Tesco?

Such was the strength of M&S – as perceived from the inside – that it believed it made its own *rules*. Consequently, as it went into the crisis its primary rule was value-for-money. It reasoned that the quality of goods that it delivered enabled it to charge premium prices. Once into the crisis, of course, the rules changed and the predominant rule became 'do not ignore the shareholder'. Crises also reveal underlying rules that have always existed and have been ignored by the players. In M&S's case this was the 'nobody is safe' rule. M&S's colossal arrogance was a clear indication that nobody in the organization knew this rule existed.

Because of its general lack of awareness, M&S also failed to realize that the *environment* in which it operated had changed, making its practices outmoded and unsuitable for survival. The intelligence function of the organization was either not operating correctly or not being listened to. In the prevailing M&S culture both were probably true. Once the crisis emerged, the intelligence function went into overdrive and bombarded the organization with the environmental information. What it showed was the environment in which previously M&S had previously been the only source now suddenly had a variety of alternatives. The alternatives were also capable of much speedier reactions to the market place. Where M&S had two seasons per year, GAP had 14. Where M&S had a seven-day restocking period, Next had 72 hours. The environment was now one of high speed, quick response and a myriad of alternatives.

As a consequence M&S had to demonstrate a whole new *skill* set. Before, M&S needed, or thought it needed, only one skill – the ability to remain stable. What it always needed, but never recognized, were skills in vision, flexibility, intelligence and responsiveness. In order for any business to grow to the size of M&S those skills must have been in place at one time and must have been finely tuned. However, complacency and apathy had dulled the skill base. M&S believed it did not need to market; as a consequence it was unresponsive. The first characteristic of crisis is surprise: M&S's antiquated processes and structure, combined with the smugness of success, virtually guaranteed surprise. M&S needed to resurrect the skills that had made it big and also add some new skills, like transparency of process and enlightened leadership, to re-invigorate the organization. Where Greenbury had stifled debate, Salsbury needed to encourage it and empower the staff at all levels.

assessment of the crisis game

As an organization M&S scores a miserable 3/10 for playing the crisis game. The crisis game is only wholly successfully played if crises are actually avoided. If a crisis occurs then you have been playing the stability or growth game badly. The biggest mistake M&S made was to panic. Many of the events that surrounded the crisis merely exacerbated the situation. Boardroom coups, massive restructuring, staff culling, head-hunting and the appointment of new financial advisers were all initiated to appease the city analysts. The changes were necessary, but it was not necessary to undertake them in such a knee-jerk fashion. M&S was still the biggest kid on the high street block with a massive resource base. Its huge, albeit damaged, brand should not have been so easily derailed by a surplus of black and grey clothing and an unusually warm September. What M&S needed during the

> the biggest mistake M&S made was to panic

crisis was leadership with the ability to restructure and refocus with the appearance of calm authority. Salsbury, while he impressed many, did not manage to exude sufficient calm authority – as the share prices shown in Fig. 13.1 indicate. They give no evidence of confidence in the revival of M&S.

Figure 13.1 Marks & Spencer's share price

The extremely high-risk recovery strategy of heavy buying, price cutting and going for market share and volume does not sit well with the brand. What was wrong with M&S was a narrow mindset that failed to recognize huge environmental changes and increased competitor success. That can only be changed by a radical alteration of corporate culture – a job that must eventually be overseen by an outsider. Salsbury cannot be that man unless he works in a genuinely synergistic manner with the new chairman.

However, what the M&S crisis game will probably show in the long term is that with a massive resource base you can afford to make mistakes, just as IBM famously did with PCs. But M&S must also understand that a strong resource base can be tempting bait for predators. Knutsford, the retail investment vehicle, continues to stalk M&S and Philip Green, the retail entrepreneur, was beaten off. The response to Green's approach once again demonstrated the M&S board's ignorance of their responsibilities to their shareholders. A simple reflection on the performance of

M&S share prices before, during and after Green's interest may have alerted more active shareholders to the possibility of better performance under a Green regime. It was active shareholder intervention that eventually forced the Mannesmann board to capitulate to Vodafone's aggressive acquisition manoeuvres. Like M&S, Mannesmann's initial reaction was defensive. Genuine commitment to shareholder value demands that any approach must be considered only in relation to the shareholders' interests.

Another crucial aspect of M&S's situation is that M&S's three largest investors are American institutions with a reputation for arranging take-overs. One of them, Franklin Resources, is considered to be obsessively focused on shareholder value. M&S must therefore play to its strengths if it is to survive. It must re-woo the great British public which, like all disaffected lovers, cannot wait to come back if only the terms are right. For M&S those terms must be no dilution of quality, reasonable pricing, fashion responsiveness and a customer-focused shopping experience. The public want to love M&S again and will do so with the right encouragement. The M&S board needs to appease both disaffected customers and shareholders – not an easy task for a relatively inexperienced team.

Post-match analysis

The appointment of Luc Vandevelde has led to positive changes such as a belated recognition that M&S is actually a brand, that it needs to be a global retailer, that it needs to be wired (hence the establishment of its Ventures outfit) and that it needs to be sensitive to both internal and external environments. However, its market capitalization is still 62 per cent below its 1997 high. This will be a long game.

the litigation game

Microsoft v the US government

This chapter is not about the Microsoft phenomenon, or even the Bill Gates phenomenon, it is about how Microsft played against the US government Anti-trust Division. The Microsoft litigation case (Civil Action No. 98-1232 (TPJ) United States of America (Plantiff) v. Microsoft Corporation (Defendant)) has taken on the same mythical proportions as that of Rockefeller's Standard Oil earlier in the twentieth century. It also revived memories of the AT&T and IBM cases of the 1970s. It provided more evidence that the real American economic god is competition because size and reputation were no protection. Its ramifications were expected by many analysts to be central to the effective functioning of the US economy.

US anti-trust law is, like its British counterpart, designed to safeguard consumers by ensuring that competition is not stifled by anyone who dominates the market. The three major pieces of federal antitrust law are the Sherman Act (1890), the Clayton Act (1914) and the Tunney Act (1974). Each element affected the government's case against Microsoft. The Sherman Act identifies two aspects of monopolistic activity – first, 'the possession of monopoly power in the relevant market' and second, 'the wilful acquisition or maintenance of that power as distinguished from growth or development as a consequence of a superior product, business acumen or historical accident'. The Clayton Act deals with 'tying arrangements' or what we would call 'bundling' strategies. The Tunney Act established judicial oversight procedures governing consent decrees entered into by the government in order to settle anti-trust cases.

Until the 1970s, anti-trust cases had largely been brought by interventionist regulators concerned with making their own reputations. In the 1970s the emphasis altered to reflect a more economics-driven approach, which argued that many previous anti-trust actions had actually harmed American business rather than aided it. It was this view that culminated in the dropping of the infamously long investigation into IBM in 1982. Since 1982 there had been a more accommodating attitude by the anti-trust authorities, especially in relation to the emergent industries such as computing. In the early 1990s, however, it became clear to the authorities that what was potentially the most powerful economic engine of the decade, the PC, was being dominated by two giants, Intel (the processing number one) and Microsoft.

The concerns of the anti-trust authorities were exacerbated by two issues peculiar to the new high-tech industries. The first was that in this business there had emerged a 'law of ever-increasing returns' – the ability to be first in the race for a technological edge enables the winner to start the race for the next innovation at an advantage. This allows a cumulative competitive advantage to build up. The second worry concerned entry barriers to the business. Simply by being so dominant, Microsoft erected impossibly high entry barriers. Any customer wishing to change to a rival product would need to spend prohibitive amounts on retraining staff or replacing software. These concepts revealed an underlying change in the competitive relationship – that innovation is as important as price for the well-being of the consumer. Therefore, even though Microsoft's activities were producing cheaper products and happy consumers they might simultaneously be viewed as restricting innovations of the next generation. The first concrete manifestation of this new thinking came in 1995 when the Justice Department blocked Microsoft from acquiring Intuit, the personal-finance software company.

simply by being so dominant, Microsoft erected impossibly high entry barriers

That should have been Gates' wake-up call. Instead, on 19 October 1998 the battle against Microsoft was joined in the District of Columbia district court. The US government, in conjunction with 19 states, alleged violations of the Sherman Act, 1 and 2, in addition to a variety of state statutes, by Microsoft Corporation. The Justice Department charged that Microsoft was engaging in anti-competitive and exclusionary practices designed to maintain its monopoly in PC-operating systems and intended to extend those practices to Internet-browsing software. Joel Klein, the Assistant Attorney General in charge of the Anti-trust Division of the Department, stated that the intention of the action was to 'protect innovation by ensuring that anyone who develops a software program will have a fair opportunity to compete'. Klein added that:

Inventors and investors cannot and will not develop and market innovative software programs if they know that Microsoft can use its Windows monopoly to block the distribution of their programs and to force consumers to buy Microsoft's competing products.

Just to make sure nobody misunderstood, Klein finally added that the lawsuit sought to 'put an end to Microsoft's unlawful campaign to eliminate competition, deter innovation, and restrict consumer choice'.

More than a year later the Judge, Thomas Penfold Jackson, delivered a 207-page document detailing his 'findings of fact' (http://usvms.Gpo.Gov). The document was damning in its condemnation of Microsoft, as its final paragraph shows:

Most harmful of all is the message that Microsoft's actions have conveyed to every enterprise with the potential to innovate in the computer industry. Through its conduct toward Netscape, IBM, Compaq, Intel, and others, Microsoft has demonstrated that it will use its prodigious market power and immense profits to harm any firm that insists on pursuing initiatives that could intensify competition against one of Microsoft's core products. Microsoft's past success in hurting such companies and stifling innovation deters investment in technologies and businesses that exhibit the potential to threaten Microsoft. The ultimate result is that some innovations that would truly benefit consumers never occur for the sole reason that they do not coincide with Microsoft's self-interest.

Three months after the Jackson findings of fact, Microsoft launched its Windows 2000 (W2000) operating system (OS). So has Microsoft moved to a position of greater market dominance? Apparently not. Although it still dominates the desktop-PC market it has only 14 per cent of the world's computer servers running on Windows NT, compared with Unix's 40 per cent. The most optimistic forecasts suggest that it will reach 30 per cent by 2003. IDC, the American market research group, estimated that the market take-up of W2000 would be slow, with many businesses waiting as long as 18 months before implementing the new OS for fear of repetitions of the technical teething problems experienced after previous launches. Even if Microsoft's own estimate of huge successes for W2000 are correct, its market share could never reach monopolistic dominance. The efforts of traditional competitors such as Sun and Novell have been increasingly bolstered by a new competitor, Linux. Linux is a free OS that has had two significant effects on the market: it has generated a multitude of start-ups, which have developed applications based on Linux into which established companies are buying, and it has secured endorsements from IBM and Hewlett-Packard. Linux is currently the fifth largest OS behind Microsoft, but by 2003 it is expected to be second.

Bill Gates disagreed with Judge Jackson, arguing that it simply is not possible simultaneously to stifle innovation and monopolize the software game. By its very nature the software game is dynamic, with new players constantly joining and changing the game. Should Microsoft or any other player ever sit back it will wither and die. Microsoft's aim has always been to dominate the market, but that is not to abuse that domination. In Microsoft's response to the findings of fact (18 January 2000)

the software game is dynamic, with new players constantly joining and changing the game

it argues that the findings 'do not affect the phenomenal competition and innovation' prevalent in the industry. The companies cited by Judge Jackson as victims of Microsoft bullying were Netscape, IBM, Compaq, Intel (the same Intel the authorities were also charging with competition violations). None of these companies has disappeared.

The Gates line was further strengthened by AOL's acquisition of Netscape in the middle of the trial. The subsequent $156 billion take-over of Time Warner by AOL has also challenged complete Microsoft dominance, since it is the area in which Microsoft is dominant (desktop PCs) that is most at risk from digital convergence and wireless application protocol (WAP). Ironically, Netscape users are now complaining of being irritated by the AOL features that are embedded in the browser. An editorial in *USA Today* (13 January 2000) shows how the attitude towards Microsoft has shifted. Referring to the attempts by Justice Department lawyers to break up Microsoft, the paper stresses that it is 'anti-competitive practices, not mere corporate girth, which threaten consumer welfare'. With AOL quadrupling its cash flow and Microsoft contracting, it is clear that dominance is not a monopoly. In such a volatile market the robust response of the other players was also entirely predictable.

Throughout the trial the market virtually ignored the possibility of negative findings. Microsoft stock actually rose by 70 per cent during the trial period. Although Microsoft shares dropped by 4.4 per cent upon the release of Judge Jackson's finding they had recovered and improved by just over 9 per cent within three months. What Judge Jackson did was to make a judgement on a snapshot of an inherently dynamic industry. He would have been better served by using a dynamic simulation model.

But if Microsoft was not guilty (not necessarily innocent) then why did it lose? Because originally Gates completely misunderstood the game. He saw only his own reality. His *motivation* was to continue developing the best product and to do this by aggressive marketing practices. The *others* were only ever divided by the maxim 'if you're not with us you're against us'. Gates tried to build *collaborative* alliances with other software players, but when that failed he re-badged them as *competitors* to be beaten. With the aid of his legal eagles he understood the stated *rules* of the game but completely misunderstood the unstated 'too fat-cat' rule. A 'let's get Bill Gates' culture built because at no stage did Gates ever demonstrate any degree of humility. As an aspiring nerd, giving hope to those disenfranchised by a macho US college culture, such confidence was attractive. In the richest man in the world it became repugnant. The *environment* was no longer one in which nerds were persecuted but one in which they were powerful, at least as they were represented by Gates. What was once perceived as youthful enthusiasm and healthy ambition was now perceived as megalomania and ruthlessness.

Gates did not have the *skills* needed to redress the situation. He needed to be patient, to be a diplomat, to be able to compromise and to be a propagandist. He also lacked tactical acumen and subtlety. Throughout the trial his lobbying tactics were crude and unhelpful. The stage-managed announcement of plans to build closer links with Congress by providing technical support to individual members was clumsy and insensitive. Prior to the trial the simple expedient of allowing PC manufacturers to remove Microsoft's browser icon from their screens could have diverted the attention of the anti-trust authorities. The company's arrogant stance emanated, according to Judge Jackson, directly from Gates himself. Microsoft had consistently demonstrated a disregard for, and probably ignorance of, the power of the anti-trust authorities. Gates did not understand the pay-back rule which simply stated says 'those you beat will wait as long as it takes to pay you back'.

It was at this low point, however, that Bill Gates recovered his credibility as a game player – he learned. He did not rush to an appeal, but instead moved quickly to remove the biggest impediment to achieving his goals – himself. He handed over the operational reins of the company to his old poker partner, Steve Ballmer, although Gates remained Chairman and took on the additional role of Chief Software Architect. It

Bill Gates recovered his credibility as a game player – he learned

was a ploy to ease the relationship between Microsoft and the Justice Department. With Gates still in place it would have been virtually impossible to reach a settlement of the case. With Ballmer leading negotiations, however, it might be possible to reach an accommodation during the relatively quiet period between the findings of fact and the final decision as to whether Microsoft had actually broken any anti-trust laws. It is particularly important for Microsoft that the judge is sympathetic to pleas not to enforce a break-up of the company. Gates is desperately opposed to the break-up, despite the fact that as separate entities the constituent parts of Microsoft would generate increased shareholder value all round. Gates does not want that; he wants Microsoft to provide the best products.

assessment of the litigation game

We give Gates a score of 5/10 as a litigation player: a mean score derived from a score of 3/10 for pre-trial and trial play and 7/10 for post-trial play. Up to the announcement of the findings of fact Gates had been totally unaware that he was involved in a game in which losing was an option. He underestimated the skills, determination and power of the other players, including the regulators. He was unfamiliar with the 'too fat-cat' rule and generally displayed an arrogance and stubbornness that merely fuelled the opposition. He failed to recognize the altered needs of the company. It was no longer a start-up, in which aggression, ambition and ruthlessness are necessary characteristics. Microsoft had evolved into a corporate giant – with consequent responsibilities to its industry and the community at large.

Post-match analysis

In April 2000 the judge delivered the damning verdict everyone had expected. Joel Klein, the government's anti-trust prosecutor, said of the verdict, 'This ruling shows that no company, no matter how powerful or how successful, can refuse to play by the rules.' Perhaps we were over-generous to Gates with his post-trial score because, even after the June break-up ruling, he is still refusing to settle and antagonizing the opposition and referee. However, if his stalling tactics pay off we may have to increase his score – do not bet against him.

the brand game

BMW and Rover

In the chapter on Marks & Spencer we commented on how absurd it was that a company of that size had only recently established a marketing department. One of the major appointments to that department was what M&S referred to as its 'brand custodian'. This was a post charged with protecting the essence of M&S, its identity. When we spoke with other corporate players they all made the same point about the centrality of the brand, although it meant very different things. Steve Ridgeway (managing director of Virgin Atlantic), for example, explained his job as 'maintaining and protecting the spirit of the company'. Clearly he viewed Virgin as a value-driven organization. Nick Fell, the marketing director of Guinness, by contrast, sees Guinness as selling a 'combination of intoxication and nurture'. What both were doing was defining the identity of their organization. In the early 1990s BMW had a very clearly defined and highly successful brand but it also had an inherent weakness in the market in which it was playing. That weakness was a lack of volume. Everybody at BMW recognized that the industry's giants – such as Ford, Fiat and Volkswagen – were hovering menacingly at their gate and that BMW needed to increase its unit production volume to somewhere in the region of two million within a decade to compete as a global player.

BMW needed to become a full-time supplier in order to maintain its position as an independent, autonomous company that retained the Bavarian-ness central to its identity. This meant that BMW needed full access to the entire product range from small cars to Rolls-Royce (which comes under the BMW banner in 2003). It also meant, at least for Bernd Pischetsrieder, the relatively new chairman of the management board, that this diversity could not occur under a single brand. In February 1994 he made the decision to acquire the Rover group from British Aerospace in order to provide the potential for growth that BMW considered essential to its survival. Despite the poor reputation of Rover, Pischetsrieder had little option to go for it, since there were no real alternatives. At that stage there was minimal disagreement with the decision within BMW. However, very quickly it became obvious that there were both strategic and tactical differences affecting the integration of what became known as the 'English patient' into the BMW group. On the strategic level Wolfgang Reitzle, Pischetsrieder's *de facto* deputy and wannabe chairman, opposed the idea of generating the necessary growth for BMW on the back of a suspect separate brand. Pischetsrieder reasoned that incorporating the Rover products under the BMW banner and building a BMW2-series, as Reitzle wanted, would dilute the exclusivity of the BMW marque.

Pischetsrieder told us there was an emotional resistance to Rover within BMW, at all levels. He also intimated that Reitzle was the lightning rod for that emotion and indeed was its champion. It was common knowledge in the industry's media that Reitzle was leaking against Pischetsrieder, so why did Pischetsrieder not sack his deputy? The answer, according to Pischetsrieder himself, was also an emotional one. Throughout our interview with him, Bernd Pischetsrieder's conversation was peppered with references to '*my* cars' and '*my* company'. When we asked point blank why he did not remove Reitzle he replied that the needs of the company were paramount and Reitzle's talent was central to its success. It was an interesting, and arguably fatal, decision.

there was an emotional resistance to Rover within BMW

In late 1998 and early 1999 it became clear that Rover's losses were enormous and were draining the entire BMW group. Losses had increased from £91 million in 1997 to £650 million at the end of 1998. Reitzle saw an opportunity to put even more pressure on Pischetsrieder and what amounted to virtual civil war broke out. The image of Bavarian calm and efficiency that had taken years to cultivate was being tarnished. The Quandt family, which controls BMW, decided to act. Their man on the supervisory board, Eberhard von Kuenheim, called a board meeting for Friday 5 February 1999. After virtually an entire day of negotiating, a short statement was issued in which neither combatant was victorious – both Pischetsrieder and Reitzle had been forced out. Joachim Milberg, BMW's head of manufacturing, had been appointed as the new chairman of the management board.

Von Kuenheim had been strengthened on the supervisory board by the support of Manfred Schoch, the deputy chairman and BMW works council chairman. Schoch in turn was able to draw comfort from his close personal friendship with the Transport and General Workers' Union's chief motor-industry negotiator, Tony Woodley. Between them, they were later to deliver a unique working-time agreement at Rover. The value of their relationship became obvious once Pischet-srieder had made two decisions. The first was to abandon the hands-off managerial approach and the second to reveal the depth of Rover's financial crises at the Birmingham International Motor Show in October 1998. The former signalled the demise of the BMW-installed Rover chairman, Walter Hasselkus. The latter signalled the need to invest in Rover at such a level that government subsidy would also be needed. As Pischetsrieder put it in his statement, 'short-term actions are required for the long-term future of the Rover group'. The most immediate 'short-term' need was for massive cost-cuts allied to increased productivity.

Pischetsrieder warned that only such drastic action could save the Mini and the R30 and that only those products could save Longbridge. Tony Woodley, the union negotiator, correctly assessed that the BMW solution would involve huge job losses and considerable wage cuts. Woodley, in consultation with Manfred Schoch, came up with a ground-breaking trade-off between future pay and working hours, involving 'annualized hours' and 'working accounts'. The deal also managed to deliver the first 35-hour week in the British automotive industry. During interviews, both Woodley and Schoch were justifiably proud of their parts in the agreement. Both Woodley and Schoch survived, but the chairman Walter Hasselkus was sacrificed, as it was he who had been charged with turning Rover around.

For Pischetsrieder there was also the vexed issue of government aid. He had been taken aback by the dismissive response to his overtures by the Secretary of State for Trade and Industry, Peter Mandelson, and wondered, in public, why BMW should be denied similar aid to that which Ford had been given. Ford had received £72 million for its S-Type project and £45 million for its mini-car. There was considerable mistrust between BMW and Mandelson fuelled by persistent, if as yet unproven, rumours of an unhealthily close relationship between Ford and Mandelson.

Following Mandelson's resignation in late 1999, his replacement, Stephen Byers, maintained the government view that BMW was overplaying the magnitude of the crisis. But as Woodley said to us, 'BMW were not bluffing, this really was the most difficult problem the car industry has faced in the last 25 years.' Byers decided to flex his muscles. He constructed a package, purportedly in consultation with Alan Milburn at the Treasury, which amounted to £118 million. The BMW board, which thought it had a deal with Byers at somewhere between £150 and 160 million, rejected the package out-of-hand. The unions subsequently brought tremendous moral pressure to bear on the Blair Cabinet and Woodley, a veteran of the old-style car-industry negotiations, began talking to the media about '50,000 job losses' and the 'devastation of a region'. Local MP Julie Kirkbride characterized the Byers' package as 'astonishingly cavalier; it seems as if [he] is playing poker with 50,000 jobs'. New Labour's Old Labour credentials were on the line and the Cabinet Office instructed Byers to stop posturing and get a deal sorted. His officials came up with a £152 million offer which BMW accepted.

In the year after the infamous dismissal of Pischetsrieder and Reitzle, Rover's losses increased from £650 million to £800 million, dragging BMW towards the abyss. Pischetsrieder decamped to VW and Reitzle to Ford's premium-brand group. During that time Milberg has re-asserted his commitment to the Pischetsrieder strategy, in which Rover was a central part. He also re-asserted Pischetreider's belated conversion to a hands-on managerial style. Rover was totally integrated into the BMW organizational structure. Most importantly, in the brand game, this included the marketing function.

At the operational level Munich people held all the key positions, including Werner Samann who replaced Walter Hasselkus as the management board member with overall control of Rover. But the financial haemorrhaging persisted, even though there nothing inherently wrong with any of the Rover models – the Rover 75 is a particularly impressive piece of engineering. The problem is that every other vehicle in the market place is also well engineered. In an interview with Andrew Lorenz of the *Sunday Times*, Wolfgang Reitzle perfectly articulated the brand game dilemma:

In the future [the auto business] will be a power game with brands where the product will always be at the core – but not the dominating factor that it was in the past. The importance of sales and marketing in the next decade will be even greater than in the last ten years. The products are increasingly at a similar level of quality. There are almost no bad cases on the market; even for mass-produced products, quality is now a given, not a matter of differentiation.

In our interviews with BMW people nobody seemed to quite grasp the fragility of the Rover brand. Admittedly the brand is stronger in continental Europe than it is in Britain and that is where 70 per cent of Rover sales occur. But it is as if, because Rover presented BMW with its only real opportunity to enter the full-line production game, BMW convinced itself that the Rover brand really was worth acquiring.

nobody seemed to quite grasp the fragility of the Rover brand

An analysis of the BMW/Rover situation made by Andrew Lorenz, the business editor of the *Sunday Times*, suggests that given all the references to poker playing and bluffing that occurred during the government-aid negotiations perhaps the best analogy would be of a series of poker tables at which a series of games were under way. Some players would play at only one table, but some at several. Stephen Byers, for example, would play in the Cabinet game, the union game and the negotiation game.

In the brand game, BMW had only one, very clear *motivation* and that was to retain the 'independence' of the company and to maintain the exclusivity of the BMW marque. Because there were so many games, there was a plethora of significant *others*. These included the British government, in the form of the formidable Peter Mandelson and subsequently the weak Stephen Byers who, if he were the centre of this analysis, would only receive a 3/10 mark. Also playing were the unions in Britain and the workers' council in Munich. The EU became a player once the aid package was referred to it, and the predators of Fiat, VW, Ford and GM were always in game. Inside BMW there were the Quandt family, Pischetsrieder and Reitzle until their demise, and Joachim Milberg after it. The stated *rules* concerned European competition law, corporate law and employee law. The unstated rules were those normally associated with negotiation games, where anything is permitted provided you do not get caught. There was also the added restriction of the Quandts' concern for integrity.

The *environment* in which the game was played was changed from that in which most of the players had been used to playing. There was enormous overcapacity in the industry, to which government subsidies only added. There were mergers, such as the Daimler–Benz/Chrysler deal, which created industry giants. There was also an increase in more limited alliances and collaboration projects, in addition to diversification into the whole panoply of automative-related services. BMW's insistence on retaining its independence in a corporate environment that was increasingly committed to shareholder value was a major obstacle to success, especially with a loss-making subsidiary that was, ironically, supposed to be its growth engine.

In the brand game the *skills* needed are those of the strategist, the propagandist and the marketeer. As Reitzle said, brand not technology will be the future differentiator. What Pischetsrieder and subsequently Milberg needed was the ability to pick an appropriately powerful brand partner and then to market it ruthlessly. The subsidiary skills they needed were those of the poker player or negotiator. They do seem to have had those skills: they outplayed Stephen Byers and played a sensible draw with the workers' representatives. We suspect they have also bluffed the EU with the Hungarian alternative to Longbridge.

> brand not technology will be the future differentiator

assessment of the brand game

BMW, mostly in the shape of its ex-chairman Bernd Pischetsrieder, is awarded 5/10 for its performance in the brand game. There is no doubt that the BMW brand was damaged by association with the sickly Rover brand. There is also continuing activity by the major predators, especially VW, Ford and GM. Milburg has stated his aim was to 'create a level of value so substantial BMW can no longer be the subject for bid speculation'. He has singularly failed to achieve that goal and the Merrill Lynch analyst Stephen Reitman has even suggested the unmentionable – that the Quandt family might have a limit to their commitment to autonomy. While Milberg endorsed the Pischetsrieder strategy for BMW's expansion and consequent survival, in retrospect Reitzle got it right. Although we will probably always see the distinctive blue-and-white quartered marque it may soon be as part of an expanded VW or GM, just as the distinctive MG marque is currently part of BMW. On 20 February 2000 the *Sunday Times* reported Joachim Milberg saying that in ten years' time BMW 'will be as independent as we are today and sell more cars than in our record year of 1999'. If anybody offers you better than even money on that prediction – bite their hand off.

Post-match analysis

We now know that our analysis was, unfortunately, accurate. Rover has been sold and will be broken up. The Rover brand was sick and BMW learned the lesson that you do not make yourself more healthy by taking on a sick partner. BMW still has a lot of playing to do if it is to survive as an independent manufacturer – past form is not very encouraging. Watch this space and also see Financial Times Prentice Hall's analysis of BMW's disastrous ownership of Rover: *The End of the Road* (2000).

conclusion

Just as we were completing the book the Vodafone/Mannesmann take-over battle was in full flow. What a great case study that would have been. It proved to us the value of this book because we genuinely felt we were better able to follow the intricacies of that particular game. Both Vodafone and Mannesmann played out, virtually in public view, their version of the acquisition game. While it differed in detail from other games, its underlying structure and principles were identical. By identifying the MORES (**m**otivation, **o**thers, **r**ules, **e**nvironment and **s**kill), analysts could have discerned a change in the game that ultimately became dominated by shareholder value. Once Mannesmann's Chairman, Klaus Essler, realized that fact he immediately became a more effective player.

Each case study in this book could have been a book in itself, but the greatest value of the cases is in applying the methodology, not judging the cases. The value of the cases we chose is their contemporaneity. As the book is published none of our players have stopped playing. Manchester United will or will not have retained the European Cup and League, but our knowledge of Ferguson's motivation tells us that, whatever the outcome, he will be preparing for the next challenge. BSkyB may not have acquired Manchester United, but its revised strategy for the expansion game, where it buys 9.9 per cent of as many Premier clubs as possible, seems to be working. Kosovo, sadly, is an ongoing dirty game with the same problems. Microsoft's problems with the Justice Department continue; Marks & Spencer is still close to crisis; and BMW is fighting a desperate independence battle. Our analyses of these case studies may not be comprehensive or even right, but the thought process demanded by our model can enable you to play the analysis game more effectively.

The theory that game playing is a basic human instinct has stood up well to our analysis. The gaming instinct is present in all game players, including the corporate variety – the fine tuning of that instinct will improve game playing in all domains, including business. Because it *is* a basic human instinct, every aspect of the book refers back to the human factor. While gaming analysis is peripherally concerned with process, technology and structure, it is *centrally* concerned with people. The learning organization is not a miraculous discovery but a simple recognition of the fact that all organizations are people organizations and, therefore, gaming organizations. What business players have to do to maximize their chances of success is to answer three questions and then subject the answers to our model. The questions are: what game do you *think* you are playing? What game *are* you playing? What game *should* you be playing. Simple, isn't it?

further reading

Chapter 1

Ashby, W. Ross (1956) *An Introduction to Cybernetics*, Chapter 11.

Ayton, P. & Arkes, H. (1998) *New Scientist*, 23 May 1998.

Baudrillard, J. (1995) *The Gulf War Did Not Take Place*, Indiana University Press.

Berne, E. (1964) *Games People Play*, Ballantine.

McDonald, J. (1950) *Strategy in Poker, Business and War*, Norton.

Nalebluff, B.J. & Brandenburger, A.M. (1996) *Co-opetition*, Doubleday.

Odean, T. http://gsm.ucdavis.edu/~odean

Rapaport, A. (1959) 'Critiques of Game Theory', *Behavioural Science and Communication*, Vol. 4, 49–66.

Von Neumann, J. & Morgenstern, O. (1994) *Theory of Games and Economic Behaviour*, Princeton University Press.

Chapter 2

Brand, D.D. *et al.* (1982) 'Improving white-collar productivity at HUD', in O'Brian, R.M. *et al* (eds) *Industrial Behaviour Modification: a learning based approach to industrial–organisation problems*, Pergamon.

Goldratt, Eliyahu M. (1994) *The Goal: a process of ongoing improvement*, North River Press.

Herzberg, F. (1968) 'One more time: how do you motivate employees?' *Harvard Business Review*, January–February, 53–62.

Maslow, A.H. (1943) 'A Theory of Human Motivation', *Psychological Review*, Vol. 50, 370–96.

Maslow, A.H. (1970) *Motivation and Personality*, 2nd edn, Harper.

Pfeffer, J. and Sutton R.I. (1999) *The Knowing–Doing Gap: how smart companies turn knowledge into action*, Harvard Business School Press, 1999.

Robertson, I.T. *et al* (1992) *Motivation: Strategies, theory and practice*, 2nd edn, Institute of Personnel Management.

Steers, R.M. and Porter, L.M. (eds) (1979) *Motivation and Work Behaviour*, McGraw–Hill.

Warr, P.D. (1982) 'A National Study of Non-Financial Employment Commitment', *Journal of Occupational Psychology*, 55 (4), 297–312.

Chapter 3

Black, A. *et al* (1997) *In Search of Shareholder Value*, FT/Pitman.

Michie, Jonathan (1999) *New Mutualism: a Golden Goal*, Cooperative Party.

Nalebuff, Barry J. and Bradenburger, Adam M. (1996) *Co-opetition*, Doubleday.

Sun Tzu (1988) *The Art of War*, translated by Steve Kaufman, Charles E. Turtle.

Chapter 4

Ashby, W. Ross (1956) *An Introduction to Cybernetics*, Chapman & Hall.

Nalebluff, Barry J. and Brandenburger, Adam M. (1996) *Co-opetition*, Doubleday.

Senge, Peter (1994) *The Fifth Discipline: the Art and Practice of the Learning Organisation*, Doubleday.

Weiner, Norbert (1948) *Cybernetics*, Wiley.

Yamada, Haru (1997) *Different Games, Different Rules,* Oxford University Press.

Chapter 5

Beer, Stafford (1995) *Brain of the Firm*, Wiley.

Gates, Bill (1999) *Business @ the Speed of Thought*, Warner Books.

Goldratt, E.M. (1992) *The Goal: a process of ongoing improvement*, 2nd edn, North River Press.

Chapter 6

Archer, M. and Cohen, R. (1998) 'Side-lined on the (Judicial) bench: sports metaphors in judicial opinions', *American Business Law Journal*, Vol. 35.

Brady, Chris (1999) 'Collective Responsibility', *Parliamentary Affairs*, 52(2), Spring.

Cattell, Raymond (1987) *Intelligence: its Growth and Structure*, North-Holland.

Clarke, Jane (1999) *Office Politics*, Industrial Society.

Goleman, Daniel (1995) 'What Makes a Leader?', *Harvard Business Review*, November–December (reprint 98606).

Goleman, Daniel (1995) *Emotional Intelligence*, Bantam.

Goleman, Daniel (1998) *Working with Emotional Intelligence*, Bantam.

Jonassen, Jan R. (1999) *Leadership: Sharing the Passion*, Management Pocket Books.

Pfeffer, J. and Sutton, R. (1999) *The Knowing–Doing Gap: How Smart Companies Turn Knowledge into Action*, Harvard Business School Press.

Chapter 7

Brady C. (1993) 'Intelligence failures: plus ça change ...' *Intelligence and National Security* Vol. 8, No 4.

Drucker, Peter F. (1999) *Management Challenges for the 21st Century*, Butterworth and Heinemann.

Hayes, R.H., Wheelwright, S.C. and Clark, K.B. (1988) *Dynamics Manufacturing Creating the Learning Organisation*, The Free Press.

Huseman, R. and Goodman, J. (1999) *Leading the Knowledge: the Nature of Competition in the 21st Century*, Sage.

Nonaka, Ikujiro and Takeuchi, M (1995) *The Knowledge–Creating Company: how Japanese companies create the dynamics of innovation*, Oxford University Press.

Pedler, M., Boydell, T. and Burgoyne J. (1997) *Learning Company Project*, The Training Agency, Sheffield.

Senge, Peter M. (1994) *The Fifth Discipline: the Art and Practice of the Learning Organisation*, New York.

Wykoff, A. (1996) 'The Growing Strength of Services', *OECD Observer* No. 200, June.

Chapter 8

Gallwey, T. (1999) *Inner Game of Work*, Random House.

Langley Paul A. and Larsen, Erik R. (1995) 'Edutainment, learning and system dynamics', *System Dynamics Review*, Vol. 2, no. 4, 321–6.

Parsloe, Eric (1992) *Coaching, Mentoring and Assessing: a Practical Guide to Developing Confidence*, Kogan Page.

Whitmore, John (1996) *Coaching for Performance*, Nicholas Brealey.

Chapter 9

Bergler, Edmund (1985) *Psychology of Gambling*, International Universities Press.

Klein, Gary (1998) *Sources of Power: How People Make Decisions*, MIT Press.

Hunt, Christopher and Scanlon, Scott (1999) *Navigating Your Career*, John Wiley.

Richer, Julian (1999) *Richer on Leadership*, Julian Richer Consultancy.

Simon, Herbert (1957) *Models of Man: Social and Rational*, Wiley.

Chapter 10

Deloitte & Touche (1999) *England's Premier Clubs: a Review of 1998 results*.

Ferguson, Alex (1999) *Managing My Life*, Hodder and Stoughton.

index